AF263207

UNOFFICIAL GUIDE
TO BECOMING THE
AVATAR

HOW TO TRANSFORM
YOURSELF TO BETTER THE WORLD

RONALD BOUDREAU

Dedication

In remembrance of my mom, June Boudreau.
Whose hard work and kindness still inspire me.

Table of Contents

Introduction

Someone once told me that nonfiction is the only genre you can really take away and learn from. I have found this to be wrong. Fiction has brought many stories where someone can learn a lesson without having to physically experience it. It creates a space where the person can see more than one point of view. Picking up a non-fiction book often leads to seeing things through just their eyes. In fictional content, each character carries a different point of view.

Growing up I was always drawn to the worlds of Pokémon, Disney, Nintendo and of course, *Avatar: The Last Airbender*. While these characters had powers and lived a life completely different than my own, there was a sense of relatability as they faced their own turmoil's. The first true connection I had with any characters was after my own mother died. Katara and Zuko became very relatable characters for me. Watching as they handled the situations and their lives helped guide me through all of my mixed emotions. Zuko became more relatable as I found myself in high school, finding that we shared a lot of the same emotions. These connections and lessons weren't going to resonate with me like they did if I read on it in a non-fiction book.

There were times as I dreamed about being a hero who could do amazing things to solve any problem. Fight bad guys and help those in need. Help those who suffer to smile again. The problem was what I thought a hero was had to be someone with supernatural powers. I created a barrier between myself and the fictional heroes I grew up watching.

Then came the moment I learned the secret to the heroes' powers; it was the small successes they had while using them. Katara could not complete a water whip unless she got each step of the form right. That's when I committed to a life of self-transformation. From there I focus on making myself better so I could one day live my best life and be a hero to those around me. Since then, I have successfully directed a play, won awards at cosplay contests, written countless manuscripts (where I can officially say one is published!) and graduated college with an Associates in Business and a Bachelor of Science in Theatre. Just to name a few of my favorite accomplishments since.

Now I am free to teach others what I have learned in my experiences. Help those around me smile. Give extra during charitable times. And most of all, I'm happy with what I'm doing in my life.

This book was created with the intent of showing people how to live their dream life. The success strategies needed to overcome obstacles. To help you face fears you never thought possible. So, one day you may do the same for someone else.

This is the knowledge to become a modern-day Avatar with all the information I have gathered from books, podcasts, and experience in my years of practicing self-transformation. Inside you will not see a step-by-step guide, but lessons to help you find your own path to a fulfilled life.

> *"When we hit our lowest point,*
> *we are open to the greatest change."*
>
> -Avatar Aang

The Beginning of Your Journey

<u>What Does It Mean To Be The Avatar?</u>

Master of all four elements and being the bridge between the worlds, is most likely, what comes to mind when you ask yourself what it means to be the Avatar. Those are just elements of the Avatar, which are steppingstones to making it to the ultimate goal of self-development and service to the world. A clearer definition of this role would be someone who puts a priority on self-development to be able to help the world.

As humans, there is a drive within ourselves to help others. As William James once said, "the deepest principle in human nature is the craving to be appreciated." To acquire appreciation, you must first please those around you with some actions, often ones that will help them in some ways. The feeling of a warm heart sings to our souls when we see a smile after making someone's day better. There is a purpose in us to help. How we want to help is an individual agenda. Each person is different. Though, the road to self-development with the aim of making an impact on the world is less traveled by.

The road to Avatarhood is a difficult one. It takes years of practice and inward-looking. Conquering your mind and past to be able to unlock power you never knew you had. Disciplining the body to work for you. Adapting to changes in social climate and culture. Each drop of blood and sweet set towards bringing out the best self to bring out the best world. As Avatar Roku put about his own training, "it was bitter work, but the results were worth it."

This book was designed to help you unleash your own Avatar power. You won't actually be able to spew fire from your hands or glide around with a makeshift glider. Reality has set us on a different course than the Avatar Universe you have grown to know. Instead, you will learn how to master the elements in terms of mastering yourself. Each element is full of knowledge, full of its own individual personality and philosophies. You will start with Earth and follow the Avatar cycle. You will learn from all of your favorite Avatars, benders, and non-benders to achieve skills you must master to become the best version of yourself.

You may be wondering, why is a requirement to be able to make a difference in the world. You could just donate money to a noble cause or volunteer time to help those in need. The part that is most forgotten is how you can do these things and keep doing them in the long term. How will you achieve the money to donate to world hunger? Will you be rested enough to help in your free time? What is the best use of your time in helping these causes? There is a line of self-discipline and growth to be able to help others. Think of the safety guidelines on airplanes; if the plane is going down, you put your oxygen mask on first, and then, help your child. You must make sure your body is able to help others. Aang knew he had to take down the Firelord to end the war and bring peace to the world. After a hundred years, it starts to become more and more urgent to end the war. Stop the bloodshed and tyranny. Aang did not rush off to the Fire Nation after being released from the iceberg to fulfill his destiny. He knew his body and mind were not ready. He would die and become useless in the dire situation the world was in. Instead, he took the time to learn and practice his bending. Becoming someone who can truly make this difference.

It will be talked more about what you will do to help serve the world later on. For now, you must come to terms with the fact that you must work on yourself to open up the possibilities of your true potential and abilities to help those around you. Choosing this path isn't the easiest thing one can do, though you will be full of joy and fulfillment when you reach the end of it. I encourage you to read on if you feel you are ready to begin the process of accepting your destiny and becoming the full-fledged Avatar you have the potential to be.

<u>Accept That You Are The Avatar</u>

The road of self-growth and improvement is not a journey everyone can do. A journey such as this brings a person to a hardworking path of determination and discipline to master the techniques needed to succeed. If success was easy, everyone would have already mastered the four elements, including the Avatar state. Only those who set their course to mastery, and stay on it, will ever reek the benefits of such life.

You must accept that you are responsible for where you currently are, acknowledge that you need to change, and then accept the hardships and accountability to be able to transform your own self. The journey to Avatarhood is one that takes time and hard work. The Avatar Universe shows that Avatars travel the world for years to learn each of the four elements. Each one starts at the basics and learns each individual style and philosophy. You master one, then move to the next.

Acceptance isn't a matter of just saying, "okay I'm going to do this, this, and this." It is a matter of fully taking responsibility for what was, is, and will be. Within this book, you will learn how to accept the trials of your life and to grow from each. You will be able to steer the course of what will be. Right now is the time to accept what is.

The present situation of the life you are living is the first steppingstone to changing your life. Come to terms that you are not where you need to be. That you need change. The future goal will not happen unless you change your present self into one who makes the actions needed to master your Avatar destiny.

While traditionally the Avatar doesn't get a choice, it is seen through Aang's journey, what happens when you don't accept this role. Aang, ultimately, felt trapped by this, that when the monk elders decided to separate him from his teacher, Monk Gyatso, he ran away and disappeared in an iceberg for a hundred years. He was resistant toward his destiny as the Avatar. It wasn't until he came to terms with it after being freed from the iceberg, that he accepted his role to master the elements and save the world.

This does not mean you must accept that you are the only one to save the world. Avatars have had a history of having friends to help. For now, accept where you are in your own life situation; whether it is money, addiction, relationships, career, and so on. Then, to accept that you can better yourself to better the situation, there are things you need to do

The first step is accepting your journey to becoming the best you can be. Master the elements talked about in this book. Then transform into the person who can better the world by bettering yourself. Accept that you are the Avatar.

Create your Avatar Affirmation

Take the time to create your own personalized affirmation to commit to your Avatarhood. Be fun, exciting, meaningful, and also bold when writing it. Think along the lines of Korra's famous line, "I'm the Avatar and you have to deal with it!" Proclaim your Avatar destiny with pride and power! Start with an "I am" statement first. Then fill in the blanks on how you are the Avatar. Write it down and put it somewhere you can see it daily. A few places to try are your bathroom mirror, desk, car dashboard, and your phone lock screen. The more often you see it the faster your brain will rewire itself to believe it.

Uncle Iroh's Wisdom

"It's time to start looking inward and start asking yourself the big questions: Who are you and what do you want?"

Iroh asked questions many people try to avoid. They try to put up a facade where they think they know, but find out later down the road they are unhappy and unfulfilled. These two questions can make the biggest difference in our journey of where we end up. If you do not establish who you are and what you want out of life, then, you will never take the road needed to accomplish such things. There will be no guide to being the authentic self. You will never be the person needed to accomplish what your heart wants to change. Take time to meditate, ponder and journal about these. As the Avatar, you will need to know what kind of Avatar you want to be, what Avatar you need to be. You will also need to figure out what you want from this journey, what it can give you in life that you have longed for.

<u>Your Nation</u>

While the Avatar is the master of all four elements, they have to come from one nation to begin with. You will discover your nation by the ten-question quiz provided. Write down your answer to each one by selecting from the provided answers.

1. You are on vacation in a new place, what is the first thing you do?
    A. Go for a walk to see what there all is.
    B. Go and find a place to relax such as a poolside or a spa.
    C. Set up the hotel room and plan out the rest of the stay.
    D. Drop off the stuff and go straight to the first attraction.

2. A close friend is going through a breakup, what do you do?
    A. Give them space.
    B. Bring them ice cream/ anything else to help cheer them up.
    C. Help them get back out there.
    D. Remind them how worthy of love they are.

3. You're job hunting, what are you looking for most in one?
    A. One with a flexible schedule.
    B. One where I can help people.
    C. One with good job security.
    D. One that is fast-paced.

4. At a party, what are you most likely doing?
    A. Sitting off to the side petting a dog.

B.   Helping the host with refreshments.
C.   Socializing with others.
D.   The first one dancing.

5. Someone is telling you a story, you are?
   A.   Silently and intently listening.
   B.   Asking questions to understand it better.
   C.   Repeating what they say to confirm you heard it right.
   D.   Starting to tell them a similar story that happened to you.

6. In the morning, which of the four activities are you most likely to do?
   A.   Enjoy a cup of coffee alone
   B.   Cook breakfast for the whole house.
   C.   Check the weather for the day.
   D.   Exercise.

7. You need to make a big decision, what do you do?
   A.   Look at all options before choosing one.
   B.   Go to others for advice.
   C.   Make a pros and cons list.
   D.   Go with the first thing you think of.

8. You are on a deadline for a project, what do you do?
   A.   Research, research, research.
   B.   Recruit people to help you.
   C.   Stick to schedule to get it done.
   D.   Get it done quickly so it's out of the way.

9. Which application on a phone do you use the most?
   A. Camera
   B. GPS
   C. Calendar
   D. Alarm

10. You don't like what you ordered at a restaurant, what   do you do?
   A. Don't tell the waiter, eat a few bites, and say you're not that hungry.
   B. Don't tell the waiter, eat it anyways.
   C. Tell the waiter, ask for a recommendation for something else.
   D. Tell the waiter and order something you know you will like.

Now that you have completed the quiz, add up how many you got of each individual number. The highest scored letter will correlate with the nation that fits you best. A = Air, B= Water, C=Earth and D= Fire.

The nation with the highest score will be the element you may find to be easier to grasp. For example, if you scored highest with Earth, you will find the Earth element easier to grasp and master. Your scores can also foretell which element you may have a harder time with. Think of it like how Aang struggled to learn Earth bending and Korra struggled to learn Air bending. It is their opposite in personality. Instead of ignoring that element, take the warning to really buckle down and focus on the material.

<u>Choosing Your Animal Guide</u>

One of the fun parts of being an Avatar is making your best friends for life, your animal guide. Aang had Appa. Korra had Nagga. Roku had Fang. Wan had Mula. Each one had an incredible bond with their animal guide. So strong that Guru Pathik could find Aang through his connection with Appa.

This step does not mean you have to go to the pet store and buy a puppy or go out and tame a wild bison, as fun as that may sound. This step is finding someone who supports you as the animal guides do. This could be a human for you. This animal guide for you, like the other Avatar's, will be loyal and supportive to you. Just as Nagga went looking for Korra after she was kidnapped by Tarlock. Fang lying by Roku to comfort him through death. Mula chose to travel with Wan when he left the Oasis. A friend who will stick by you through thick and thin.

An animal guide for you might look different for you than it does for others. There is always moral support with encouraging words. They might be the listening ear you need to think through your challenges and frustrations. There may be times this person will drop everything to help you with tasks such as travel, as we have traditionally seen animal guides such as Appa does for Aang. They could help you with a variety of tasks, as Nagga would sniff and track on command for Korra. The possibilities are limitless as they help and support you throughout your journey.

Keep in mind, you don't necessarily get to choose who this is. Just like the sky bison, they choose you. There is no forcing of a connection. Instead, the animal guide must want to support you. Forcing someone to fill this role will only give you false support. You will be surrounded by anxieties about keeping your support and wondering if you are even worth it. It will only give you doubt. A true connection will give you unconditional support, someone to catch you when you fall.

You will know who this is as you go through your journey. It is the person whose energy matches yours. You will feel safe around them and able to be your authentic self. There will be no doubt in the connection you have with this person. Your journey will be a part of their journey and you will grow together.

Do not mistake this guide as an accountability partner. Accountability is the job of your masters and friends, not the guide. The relationship is not the same. Masters are there to make you better. Guides are there to support you in your journey to get better. Appa never stopped Aang from goofing off. Appa didn't stop Aang from running away from the air temple. Appa stuck right by Aang no matter the circumstance. A best friend who will be there for you until the end.

Take your Animal Guide a step further.
One of the exciting things about the Avatar Universe is the assortment of animals. You have flying bison, dragons, badgermoles, polarbeardogs, platypusbears and many more. Bring the fun to your own animal guide! Assign an animal to them in your head. (They might not understand that well if you tell them they are a turtleduck) Think of what Avatar animal they are based on their personality. Are they gentle like a sky bison? As fierce as a dragon? Maybe, energetic like a polarbeardog? The sky's the limit!

<u>Find Your Teachers</u>

The best place to get to where you want to be is to seek out those who have already mastered what you are after. Avatars are no exception, for each element they seek out a new master and learn from them until they have mastered it themselves. Only those who have mastered what you want to learn will lead you on the right path. You would not go to the Fire Lord with a question about cabbage, you would instead go to the cabbage merchant. Someone who doesn't grow, love, and sell cabbages won't know as much as the man who keeps traveling with carts full of the vegetable.

We watched Aang travel all around the world to find his masters. This does not mean you have to travel across the world and study under someone. With today's technology, you can virtually connect to those who can teach you the stuff you need to master, even things beyond what is taught in this book. Teachers can be local even, such as a friend or parent. You can pay them or find someone who will do it for free. It doesn't matter who the person is, as long as you can learn the subject from them. Remember, Zuko was a dangerous enemy to Aang before he became his firebending teacher.

You will need many teachers on this journey, those who have mastered a specific area you want to conquer. You may find someone who is great with making sales, though you may not want to go to them for everything. Spread your knowledge vastly as you will find a multitude of ways to think. Imagine you are in a position like Aang was when he didn't want to take the Fire Lord's life to solve the hundred-year war conflict. While you may not be in as crucial of a circumstance, you will find you are at a crossroads finding the right path of action to align with your own values. Aang did not just stop at voicing his concern to his friends. He was led to contact his past lives and consult more than just his most recent past life, Roku. He went through an entire cycle of searching for the right knowledge to keep his values and save the world. In the end, he found the advice of a teacher he didn't even think of, a Lion Turtle, where he was inspired with the idea of taking away his bending instead of making Ozia pay the ultimate price of death.

You will find that his past lives helped in other circumstances. Roku helped teach Aang about the comet as well as how it is still good in the Fire Nation. In Korra's life, Aang came to help her learn how to bring back a person's bending after it was taken away. Kyoshi learned much from Kuruk and Yanchen about their past and how it is currently affecting the world. Each teacher you bring into your life will teach you what they can, though the more teachers you have the greater knowledge and perspective on the world.

Teachers, though, must be physical persons that can guide you in real time. Many tools such as books, videos, and podcasts can only help suggest knowledge. Think back to when Katara stole the water bending scroll from the pirates. The images on the scroll taught her and Aang the water whip, though Katara could not do it right away. She practiced and could not figure out what was wrong with her form. When the gang arrived at the Northern Water Tribe, we saw Master Paku instruct and critique to help his students perform better. A Teacher can do more than what a prerecorded lesson can. A teacher can point out the small mistakes and help you fix them to make a perfect mastery of the element. Imagine you are reading a book on how to meditate, the book can't look and see if you are slouching or check to see if you are breathing correctly. A teacher can and will take moments like those to guide you and instill the knowledge in you for the rest of your life.

<u>Follow The Process</u>

Water. Earth. Fire. Air. We have heard Katara say those four words in that order hundreds of times. This is the path laid out to go through and master. Each one has its own identity, philosophies, and techniques. The Avatar does not move on to the next element until it masters the one before it. It is not a matter of mastering being the Avatar, it is a matter of mastering the elements to become the Avatar.

Becoming an Avatar is a process. There are years of training involved. You start with the first element, which in this book is Earth. You start from there and build upon it from the bottom up. You don't skip all the way to bending huge boulders. You start with a single small stone. You master the stances and condition yourself to overcome the challenges you will face. You go through the motions daily, adding on once you are ready. Until you are eventually to a place where you can surpass your teacher. Then you start again with the next element.

Rushing through your training will not make the product come faster. Remember Aang when he started learning fire bending from Jeong Jeong. Not only was Aang jumping over two elements, he needed to master beforehand, but he was impatient to work with the flames during the actual training. Jeong Jeong had him practicing his breathing and control over the ember on the leaf before he dealt with flames. Aang did not follow the fire training process. Instead, Aang created a flame against his teacher's wishes. He played with it and ended up creating a disaster as he burned Katara's hands.

Aang focused on the product alone. When he had it in his hands, literally, he did not have the knowledge and power to control it. It's like trying to solve a calculus problem before you even learn to add two plus two. Trying to write a book before you even know how to write. Building a fire before you even know how to put it out. A process is to teach you how to establish the skills needed to get the end product. An Avatar who does not know the roots of their bending power cannot expect to become a powerful full-fledged Avatar.

Let's take into consideration another Avatar who had patience issues when learning an element. Korra was bull-headed on learning the process of airbending. She used roots of another bending, trying to force it out as if it was a flame ready to strike someone down. Instead of taking in the meditation process and focusing on the exercises meant to teach her the flow of air, she became frustrated and impatient. She even at one point just yelled air bend as she tried to shoot air to strike down a newspaper with Lin Beifong on it. We also saw her just run in headfirst and burn down an ancient Air Bender training obstacle. There was only the expectation that the Avatar can airbend, but she had not yet created a single puff of air. Her focus on the product blinded her on the key to getting it, the process that Tenzin was laying out for her.

Take the time needed to master the elements talked about in this book. Skipping out on one too early may lead to the crumbling of your hard work. When you learn more about this in a later part of this book, build and master the roots before you go into advanced practices. There is a lot to uncover in your journey to becoming an Avatar. People will show small interest in what you can actually do once you have mastered it but will want to hear all the stories of you overcoming the journey to getting where you are.

Uncle Iroh Wisdom

"You are going through a metamorphosis, my nephew. It will not be a pleasant experience but when you come out of it, you will be the beautiful prince you were always meant to be."

When Iroh says this to Zuko, he is informing him that the process of good change will not always be fun. It can be gruesome and tiring at times. But that is what creates the best change. If you undergo a difficult process, you will come out stronger and wiser than you were before. The best outcomes come from pressures in a journey, embrace them so you can become the person you were always meant to be.

Focus On Your Own Legacy

Imagine in The Legend of Korra when Tenzin is walking through the fog of lost souls trying not to be influenced to lose his mind from the spirit fog, where people become fixated on their most vulnerable moments in life. He handled his situation by talking to himself, saying, "Remember who you are, Tenzin, you are the son of Avatar Aang, you are the hope for future generations of airbenders, the fate of the world rests on your shoulders." Then spiraling into a debate of whether he will fail or already has. Without realizing it, though, he was already losing his mind. He became an overcomer with his father's vision and work that he strayed from who he was. When the spirit of Aang came before him, Tenzin let out his regrets and feelings of failure. Haunted by the fact that he isn't as spiritual as he should be. Overloaded with the burden of making the Air Nation the same as his father's stories. Ultimately saying that he would never be the man his father was.

Aang's response was the reminder we all need to remember as we choose between paths people choose for us and those we choose ourselves. Aang agreed with Tenzin by saying "You were trying to hold a false perception of yourself. You are not me and you should not be me. You are Tenzin." A reminder that you are not your parents, ancestors, friends, mentors, or anyone else in the world. You will never be them. Become only you and create your own legacy.

Your legacy is what you want people to remember you for, you mark on the world and the hearts of others. If your parents are doctors, it does not mean you must go down the same path. If you feel your calling is to become a speaker on health issues, then that is what you must do. No matter how hard you try, you will never have the same life and accomplishments as your parents and be fulfilled and happy.

Look at each Avatar, none of them is exactly the same. Not even Avatars of the same element. Take Korra and Kuruk for example. Kuruk was a free spirit, keeping his more serious Avatar duties such as dealing with spirits privately. Korra, on the other hand, is very rash and vocal, always looking for an opportunity to bend and show her power to solve a problem. Both water benders from the same reincarnation line.

We see this same difference in Avatar's legacies throughout the cycle. Looking back at Kuruk, we see how Kyoshi questioned how he was so different from Avatar Yanchen. Yanchen actively brought peace in her legacy, inspiring many in her lifetime and after. Then after her was Avatar Kuruk, who again was much more carefree and ended up dying fairly young for an Avatar- where much of the world doesn't know of his own work dealing with angered spirits from the Yanchen era. No circumstances will ever be the same. Kyoshi couldn't even replicate the legacy of Yangchen, who she looked up to. She had her own circumstances and callings as an Avatar.

Your legacies will be the things people say at your funeral, what they write about you. Things like accomplishments and values. Traits that relate to your purpose. The *why* in your life to go through this journey. The reason you want to change the world and become the best version of yourself. Ask yourself what driving force you feel the urgent need to follow. Take time to think about it, journal it out. Korra didn't know her legacy at first. We saw her go through her training with just the goal of becoming a fully realized Avatar. Then once air benders started showing up, we saw her take on the task of helping grow the nation by traveling to recruit them. Later, when she saw that it wasn't her true calling, she found herself steered to help democratize the Earth Kingdom with Prince Wu. In a matter of about four years, we see her legacy go everywhere. You will find yours, it will take time and it will come to you as you go throughout your journey. But it will only come to you if you actively look for it.

Journal questions on your Legacy

Take the time to write out with a pen and paper your answers to the following questions.

-What talents am I good at that I can use to help others?

-What talents am I passionate about?

-What does the world need right now?

-What causes am I passionate about?

-Why do I want to make a difference in the world?

-What do I want people to say about me at my funeral?

-What kind of world do I want to leave for the Avatar after me?

How will you establish your legacy? Action. You need to do the work more than you need to do the talk. If anything, don't do the talk. Take a full focus on your training to use what you learn for your desired impact. We talked about Legacy earlier on for that purpose. You will have a drive to learn from everything as you begin to organize your newfound knowledge and skills to fulfill your purpose in life.

Uncle Iroh's Wisdom

"Is it your own destiny? Or is it a destiny someone else has tried to force on you?"

This journey you are about to go on is not anyone else's but your own. If you do something just to make one person happy with your life, then you are not choosing your own path. You can still gain the power of the Avatar, though your legacy will not be yours. Choose what you want to stand for and do with your life. Following a narrative that someone else created will not bring you ultimate fulfillment, but instead, leaves you with regret.

Your Team Avatar

Being the Avatar may seem like a solo job at first glance. In reality, it is a team effort. Look back at past Avatar's friends. Aang had close friends such as Katara, Sokka, Toph and Zuko travel with him. Korra had Mako, Bolin, and Asami. Kuruk had Kelsang, Jianzhu and Hei-Ran. Even Kyoshi had Rangi and the Flying Opera Company. They never had to go through their duties alone.

As you go through your journey, find your Team Avatar. Don't think of it as a lineup you get to choose from. Your friendships will grow organically over time. Think of when Asami was introduced to Korra. At first, Korra's jealous feelings did not want her on the team. Though over time, they bonded and became closer. Asami ultimately became a valuable member of the team as she fought alongside Korra.

Your Team will most likely be an array of people. Not many Avatar teams have repeating benders. Friends from different walks of life can give you opinions that may have never occurred to you before. Embrace this in your team. If it makes it easier to label the different types of people in your team, assign them a character from Aang's team, or any other Avatar's. If you have someone who comes from a place of wanting to make social change and make a difference for minorities in the world, consider labeling them Katara. Then, when you get someone who leans towards a more tactical approach to world issues, you may have found your Sokka. The idea is to surround yourself with different methods of problem-solving.

Uncle Iroh's Wisdom

"There is nothing wrong with letting people who love you help you. Not that I love you, I just met you."

It can be seen that Iroh experiences love for all people in the end. He finds the good in them and strives to help them. Beyond that, it is okay to ask for help and to let someone help you on your journey. You can't do everything yourself, even if you are the Avatar. When people help you, it isn't necessarily because they don't think you can do it, but they want to help you reach your goal easier and see you shine.

Earth

<u>What Is Earthbending To Us?</u>

Looking back at the first earthbenders, the badgermoles, we can see the element in action as a manipulation to help them guide their way through tunnels by creating new ones where needed. All done by blind animals. In a sense, we will also be blind to our own earthbending material. What we will be creating will not be a physical structure, but a metaphorical one. Being aware and capable of manipulating this element will help elevate us from those who seek to destroy us, giving us a place to fall and rise back up to.

The grand goal of earth bending is creating and maintaining a foundation. You will be given tools in this element to build your own. Think of it as the time Toph was taught to use her body to see what was around her, to manipulate the earth particles using the vibrations around her. The badgermoles taught her the connection in all things, how to grasp the Earth particles to manipulate it, the power needed within herself to move more and more rock. It's seen later through Toph training Aang that it is all about the foundation of the body. Aang could not move a rock with a poor stance. A strong stance, rooted to the ground, and using every muscle is the only way to budge a boulder.

We see this throughout the Earth Kingdom as the land is all centered around one city, Ba Sing Se. There reigns the monarchy in the heart of the city. The status of the Earth Kingdom was based on that single city, as long as it was free, then the kingdom was free. The foundation of the Earth Bender's native land.

The journey ahead is to build the foundation with methods of earth bending. You will have to master stability, accountability, and concrete your values. These are some of the trials you will have to conquer in order to build a strong foundation. One that can hold your life in balance even during the hardest of times. Physical things may be easy to lose, though a person's foundation will keep him on track to regain what was lost.

Earth bending is purely the first steppingstone to achieving full mastery of oneself. You cannot master advanced techniques and do miraculous work without mastering the basic roots of a skill. You will be able to do much by mastering this element. You will be more aware of what you want from life and how you will achieve it. Mastering the first element is always the hardest. You must first break from the old dead roots to grow new ones, but as they are already entangled into the ground, it won't be easy. You must have patience and determination. Once you master this, you will see your life already mastering the other elements. And if you fall while learning the other elements, you will always have this one to help pull you up to try again.

The Characteristics Of Earth Benders

Before throwing you out into the training arena, let's look at *who* earth benders tend to be. People who come to mind are most

24

likely Toph, King Bumi, Bolin, Heru, and Lin Beighfong. Benders that show strong force with their body and stature. A determination that is difficult to break. Grounded in their ways and how they see the world. Stubborn, you could also call them.

Stubborn should not be taken as a negative trait in this context, though. Stubborn is the driving force to not give in. Not losing sight of hope. Breaking boundaries that were said to be unbreakable. To strive for a noble cause that they deem themselves worthy of fighting for. All of these can be seen as being stubborn in a productive and positive way.

Toph inventing metal bending is a prime example of this stubbornness. Metal bending had never been done before, yet this small blind girl trapped in a metal box was able to turn the tides of the possibilities for the bending's future. She pounded furiously, over and over, craving escape from her captors. The two men who captured her even egged her on by claiming that she could not bend metal. Toph got to a place where she stopped and felt the Earth particles within the metal and was able to do the first-ever incident where someone had bent metal with their earth bending.

Looking at Toph's spectacle, we don't see how her stubbornness of not giving up in a negative context. It was what drove her to find the answer to her freedom. Even in your own life, you can find times where your stubbornness helped for good. Maybe it was going to multiple stores to find that one thing that would make someone's day or a long night of research for a project. It doesn't have to be the negative stubbornness where you refuse to do something out of spite of someone else.

Stubbornness is a trait that can hold people to the greatest power and achievements, though it can also be a downfall as you fail to see the faults in your life. There will be times when you need to reevaluate your life, though a good foundation will bring you back to what is most important. Lin Beifong comes to mind when thinking of this. This stubborn, steadfast woman was notorious for standing her ground on her beliefs. It took her nearly 30 years to come to terms with her family squabbles and to realize that her relationship with her sister and mother is more important than the grudges that she holds. She needed to let go of the thought of who they were back in the past.

Earth benders, you will see, have a strong awareness of their surroundings. The obvious example would be Toph, who cannot see with her eyes, but she is the one to warn the group when someone is coming. Many times she can pinpoint who it is. The technicalities of the element lead these benders to focus on the small particles in the rock. Even in instances in metal, they can find the more refined particles that are Earth and manipulate each one to do their bidding. It's only a matter of time for an earth bender to be able to hone in on the smaller, more refined particles inside of platinum.

This trait taught inside this art will help you as well on your journey. You will see many times on this path where things will change and other doors will open for you. You will see things about yourself that you have never known or realized before. Use that knowledge to form your foundation and master the element of Earth.

The knowledge you will find, at times, will be difficult to face and continue. This is where the character of an Earth bender is tested and shows their own strong will. The laboring practice of this element can bring a bender to want to give up. We saw this in Avatar Aang when Toph began to teach him. The intense training and force needed can be immense at times. Though the will of an Earth bender helps them continue on their journey.

Entering this journey will test your own character as you continue down the path of Avatarhood. Learn from the character of the benders before you. Take what you need from the life of our favorite characters, especially in times of mastering the elements.

Tear Down Your Current Foundation

Imagine building a new foundation for a house, but it is on top of an old discarded one. There was no removing it and leveling the land, instead, they started building it right on top of it. How do you think that house will hold up? The same goes for your own personal foundation.

Now is the time to throw out what you know and start on a clean slate, taking in everything that is presented to you. In the book, *Zen in the Martial Arts,* Joe Hyams recalls when he first asked Bruce Lee about learning Jeet Kune Do. The famous martial artist took the opportunity to recall a story told by his own Sifu. The story went thus; a professor sought out a Zen master to ask about Zen. During the visit, the professor was caught up in showing off his own knowledge on the subject, the master went to fill up the professor's cup with tea until it was full and continued to let it overfill, eventually causing the professor to tell him that no more would go in. With this, the Zen master then said, "like this cup, you are full of your own opinions and speculations. How can I show you Zen unless you first empty your cup?"

This journey is no exception to this story. You must throw out your own internal beliefs and opinions to be able to grasp the making of a new foundation. Building on a foundation that was built with a different goal will give no space to the new material that you need for the strong foundation you need to fulfill your Avatarhood. The step to be taken now is to accept what you must do. Take time to journal through the emotions to do so. Write reminders around you to take all of this in and to trust in the process. This foundation will not disappear overnight, though over time as you start to build a new one, you'll hardly realize when it does leave.

Take a moment to reflect on Aang's journey to learn to earth bend. The mentality and strength needed to move a rock are different from what is required to move air. Aang, when faced with learning earth bending, did not let go of the air bender mentality. He stuck with the avoid mindset he was taught when learning air. While bending is connected in the end, Aang had to let go of what he knew and assumed he knew to learn from scratch. This was the only way he was going to be able to take in the teachings from Toph and master, earth bending.

Journal Questions

Take time to journal through what you need to let go of so that your cup will be empty.

- What does my foundation currently look like?
- Why could holding onto this hinder my journey?
- How will I prepare myself to empty my cup before working on my journey?

Uncle Iroh's Wisdom

"Failure is only the opportunity to begin again. Only this time, more wisely!"

When you fail, it doesn't mean to give up or that you suck. It means you get another chance to do it again, this time with the knowledge that you didn't have before. When faced with failure, take it as a win. This is how people learn, not by success. The new chance to do it right is a gift to be able to do something past expectations. It is a chance to prove that you can do something even if it isn't the first try.

Building Your Foundation: Finding Your Omashu

You must grow your roots first before you can grow upward. This will be the start of your foundation training within the earth element. The approach to this will be like a traditional earth bending stance, low to the ground and working its way up. First, we will learn to place our feet in a sturdy position to not only create power with our progression of this journey but to also be able to hold us to endure the trials that will surely come up.

Think of this as bamboo. Bamboo is a plant that will take two to three years to show any progress physically. In those few years after being planted, the seed is preparing itself with nutrients to be able to grow fast and tall, letting its roots dig deep into the soil around it. Once the two to three years are up, the growth of the bamboo skyrockets as it will reach its full height in a matter of a few weeks. Without the roots it produced in those few years, the bamboo would never be able to stand as tall as it does.

To start this process, you will need paper and a writing utensil. Journal through important questions to find your destination. This is the opportunity to find what is known as your North Star. Traditionally, the North Star was used to follow with the certainty that the person was going north. With it, they could find their way before GPS or maps. The one you are about to create will lead you to the end destination of what you want in your Avatarhood.

King Bumi demonstrated this when his city, Omashu, was captured by the Fire Nation. While he wanted his city free of the Fire Nation, he also wanted to make sure his citizens were safe in the process. Instead of insinuating violence, he chose to surrender until the solar eclipse where he could take it back easily. Even when Aang came to rescue him and ask for him to teach him Earth bending, Bumi stood fast with his eyes on the true goal he wanted to fulfill. He understood that he would not get what he truly wanted if he left with Aang. With that, he told Aang to find a different teacher. This is the power a North Star, or Omashu, can have on someone. From here on, this concept will be referred to as your own Omashu.

Journal Questions
- What am I good at?
- What do I love doing?
- If money was no object, what would I be doing?
- If I could solve one problem in the world, what would it be?
- What do I want my life to look like in…. (Career, Health, Finance, Relationships and Spiritually)

From the journaling questions, create a personal statement about your Omashu. This will be essentially your personal statement on top of a resume. You want to claim your purpose for what you are striving for. There is a lot that you have unraveled to be aiming for, so don't limit it to one sentence. Use 3-5 sentences to write out your Omashu. In those sentences, be honest about what you want. Keep this somewhere you can see it often. You can't stray from this if you are constantly looking at it to follow it.

Uncle Iroh's Wisdom

"Protection and Power are overrated. I think you are very wise to choose happiness and love."

While protection and power may help you have the latter, it isn't always the way to go. Know that sometimes you need to choose what makes you happy instead of what only guarantees a safety net. Safety nets do not promise you happiness or love or even fulfillment for that matter. But you can find protection and power in happiness and love. Everything will work out better if you choose what makes you happy and make that work into the grand scheme of things. No one likes being stuck in a job that they hate.

<u>Building Your Foundation: Your Secret Tunnel</u>

Once you know what your Omashu is, you will need to plan on how to get to it. Luckily, Chong, the nomad gives us this answer in his song, Secret Tunnel. "Built a path to be together." The tale of the two lovers traveling underground into changing tunnels to be together is another example of the power of having an Omashu (Ironically, Omashu was named after them). Their Omashu was their love for one another and to be together. They sought their way into the underground pass to go through tunnels built by the badgermoles to reach each other.

Now, you must make your path. Like the Badgermoles, you will be creating your own tunnel. This is a flexible motion that can be redirected in time as life happens. Think of yourself inside the mountain navigating the secret tunnel, you must navigate your way out even though the course is constantly changing. This is how life can be. But the goal is to get to your Omashu.

Before we do the actual path forming part, it should be clear that you cannot just think about it and keep the answer in your head. You must write it down with pen and paper. Form it into a physical being just as earth bending is intended. A solid physical foundation. Typing this on computers and phones will not give you the solidarity of this foundation. It is easy to hide information from yourself on technology. To mindlessly do something and not pay attention, physically writing information down will help you retain it as you are engaging your brain more, ultimately making the information a higher priority for it to remember.

Once you are ready with your material, it is time to start forming it with your plan to reach your Omashu. Work backward, starting with writing down your ultimate goal. From there, you will break it down into smaller goals that will help form the bigger one. Take for example Avatarhood, the ultimate goal is to become a full-fledged Avatar. The smaller goal would be to learn the four elements-each one with its own goal. From there, let's say earth bending is the first one of those goals you will be tackling- you will then plan the steps to mastering that element.

The timeline of your plan should be relevant to your own life and the goals you have. If you have a busy life with less time to devote in a day, then focus on how to work on the minimum each day. Those with more open schedules may be able to plan more in a small amount of time. The idea is to create a track to stay accountable to. Knowing when to work on your goal to your Avatar hood will be a key steppingstone in following through with your journey.

What to do in each time frame will also be a major step in making this plan. Write down a list of what you need to accomplish to reach the ultimate goal. Do not get overwhelmed here, this is merely to help get it down on paper. Now, circle the three to five most important. These are your priorities to focus on. Order them in a way that makes sense to the goal. You will not work on all of these at once. It is recommended that you only work on one at a time.

Looking at the process of Toph teaching Aang, it can be seen how the process can be broken down. Aang's first day of learning to earth bend started with him inquiring what move he would learn first while naming highly advanced fighting moves. Toph slows him down and tells him they will start with him just moving a rock. As Aang struggles with the initial movement of a rock, Toph backs it up to his mindset. He knows the stance, but he is not being rigid and tough like the rock before him. Toph brings him through multiple different exercises to open him up to stand his ground, getting him out of his natural airbending nature of avoiding. Later, when Aang stands his ground against a Sabretooth Moose Lion, Toph takes that energy to bring him into overdrive to face the problem like an earth bender. At that moment, Aang is able to move a rock for the first time, now having mastered a new skill that is needed to earth bend. While he is able to move earth, Toph stops him before freeing Sokka, knowing he wasn't ready for a higher-level move that could end up harming someone.

Creating your secret tunnel will bring you too many new discoveries about yourself. You may think you are ready for a step when really you must go back and master something else to move on. Evaluate the tunnel as Toph evaluated Aang during his first day. Do not move forward if something is wrong, take that detour to be able to get to where you want to be.

The Ground Rules

As you are planning and preparing for your journey, you will have to establish your own ground rules. These will be what you are going to play by to stay true to your foundation. These are your values essentially. These ground rules will not only keep you true to the vision you have for yourself but can also have the impact of driving you to continue on in your journey.

There is no right answer to what ground rules you should set. It is going to be whatever is true to you. If you find that your family is of high value, then use that to keep yourself involved with them as much as you can through this journey. Use them as a drive to continue on, do it for them. Imagine the life your family could have if you follow through with your Avatarhood. The influence you could have on your kids by showing them to follow their dreams and what that can accomplish. While this journey will take time away from them, it won't take all of it from them. You are setting out on this journey to create a better life. Once you achieve a full-fledged Avatar status, you will have the new freedom to use with your family as you never were able to before.

Other values can be things such as honesty. Make sure you are honest throughout the entire journey. Never to mislead someone and to be open about the truths of everything that happens. Drive on the dream of showing people that honest good people can reach the top. Miraculous things can happen when you stick to your ground rules. Good things seem to come in time to them after sorting out everything that isn't useful on the journey.

While ground rules are important and should be followed at all times, you are allowed to change them as time goes by. This does not mean you can just throw them all out when you choose not to follow them. This is an option when you find a ground-rule more attuned to your end goal. This could look like a couple of different ways. One way is that you can choose to add a new ground rule to your list and the second is you refine one of the current ones.

Adding a new rule can be seen as helpful. Realizing a new rule that will help keep you on track to your Avatar hood can be a blessing. The danger here is having too many rules. Remember how Toph felt trapped with too many rules. No rule was there to harm her but to help protect her. Limit them to the big few. A top three would be the best approach. Make a list of rules and group them together if that is easier. The idea is to not block yourself so much that you don't feel like you can do anything or that anything you do will end up hurting you. It can get overwhelming. Stick with 3-5 at most.

Refining a rule can be helpful in making it clearer what you want to do. If you have ground rules such as family, honesty, and justice already in place, and you are thinking about how you value kindness, you could group it with an existing one. For instance, you could group it with honesty and make that rule be a character- where you value a character of a person and how they approach situations and people. This will help the list stay small and not overwhelming.

Do not remove a rule unless you are more certain that Azula is crazy. If you think that a rule is not serving you at all or that it is actually harming your progress significantly, then, consider fixing it to suit you better or get rid of it. The caution with discarding a rule is the idea of giving up on it. If you find that we have honesty as a ground-rule, but you find yourself not being honest to people, getting rid of it does not solve the problem. That only shows that you are human and that you need to practice that ground rule to follow it. Getting rid of the rule would teach the mind that the rules are optional. In the case of this foundation, they are not. Nothing in a foundation is optional as it holds the whole building together.

Journal Questions
- What do I look for in a person?
- What do I expect of myself?
- What do I need to do to get to my Omashu?
- What is my list of ground rules so far? (Make it as long as possible right now)
- How can I condense them down to only a few? Do any of them have something in common?

Maintain Your Stable Stance

When you see a foundation at work, you see stability. This does not come from just throwing all the materials together. Your body will not be stable just by going into a stance once. You must practice the stance and build it in an order to reach certain stability. Make yourself as stable as the boulder that survives a hurricane. Be as strong and steady as the Grand Canyon after years of erosion. This step is essential to your foundation as it will hold you up during times of hardship.

Stability in your foundation will look similar to a boulder facing the elements. When a situation arises to test you, this will kick in and bring you through with what you know you should do. Without it, you could give in to going an easy way that goes against your ground rules, totally abandon your secret tunnel, and miss your Omashu.

Let's take a look at the Fire Ferrets for a moment. This team emphasized the importance of teamwork as they covered each other and gave openings to score some points. It can be assumed that teamwork is hugely important to the Fire Ferrets and could be put as one of their ground rules. During the tournament, we see examples of what happens when a ground-rule is abandoned. When Korra, Mako, and Bolin all acted in the love triangle created in the episode *The Spirit of Competition,* the feelings of hurt and jealousy all overtook the situation. The game, after Bolin saw Korra and Mako kiss was a disaster as no one worked together. No one really trusted each other or wanted to have their backs. After a close call to almost being all knocked out during a round, Korra steps in to pep talk them all back into teamwork mode. Once remembering their value towards their teamwork, they sprung back quickly and took the win.

This shows not only how lost we can be when we break a ground rule, but it also shows the power it can have once it's in the playing field. When entering the match, they enter into their philosophies as a team, which includes their teamwork. They entered with grudges towards each other, deciding that they can handle the match on their own. The thought of covering each other and paying attention to the other's plan of attack never crossed their mind. Instead, there was an argument and the fall of the team. As soon as they snapped out of this and remembered to focus on their teamwork, we saw a completely different team that led to a beautiful knockout.

Building stability for you won't look like Rangi ordering Kyoshi to hold a horse stance for hours. Stability will come in the form of other endurance activities. The most encouraging way is to participate in a routine. This doesn't have to mean doing the same things every day all day for the rest of your life. This means to do the things you don't really always feel like doing.

Morning routines are a great place to start. Chances you already have a morning routine, it's just not one you controlled to happen. This may be hitting the snooze a few too many times, running late, and skipping breakfast, and being rushed into your day. Instead, choose a set of 3-5 things to do in the morning that will set you off on the right foot. Start with a wake-up time without any snooze buttons. You chose to wake up at that time the night before, create stability by going through with it every morning. The rest of the morning can look how you want it as long as you plan out beneficial tasks. Popular routine options include a healthy breakfast, exercise, meditation, journal, alone time, prepping meals, and family time. Your morning will be entirely up to you.

Keeping up with something even when you don't feel like it will have more benefits than you can imagine as tasks, like sending an email and taking out the trash seem to be easier if you start the day on a good note. The morning routine will prepare you for the day to take everything on more calmly and efficiently. Look back at your rushed mornings and go through what those days were like. What was your anxiety level? Energy level? Could you focus well or were you everywhere? Did you get everything done on those days? Was it all done correctly? What was your average mood and outlook on the day?

Negative starts to the day will throw the body off balance immediately. When you are off-balance, you are more likely to go against your ground rules. Think back to Sokka when he was trapped in a hole, accompanied by a small sabretooth moose lion cub. Sokka became very hungry. In his hunger, he made promises to the universe that he would never eat meat again if he was freed from the hole. Moments after Toph earth bent Sokka out of the hole, he began to ask if they had any meat. The hunger imbalanced him so much that he began to bargain to go against one of his own values, which in his case is meat. Once he was free, and still hungry, he dismissed the notion that he even made that promise and went straight for his most desired thing, meat.

In your own life, think back to when you were hungry. Not just hungry though, starving and you know you can't eat right away. What was your mood, attitude, focus level, and decision-making process like? There is a reason the term hungry was formed. The imbalance you have is a basic need that needs to be kept up with or else, you can lose your control. A sudden urge for food will make you rush through situations, say more harsh words, and let you miss details that could have helped you in your journey. To avoid imbalances, set up your day in a way that you make sure you hit the things that will help your body and mind flourish. Make sure foods your body responds well to are available at correct times, adequate sleep, time to work on the mind, time to work on the body, time with those you love. Sokka may have been stuck when his imbalance happened, but you have all the time you need to plan ahead and create a routine that will help you hit your goals.

A routine also has an effect on us where certain times will become automatic to us to do what we have planned. If you choose to watch TV with the family every night at 8 o'clock, then once it hits that time, your body is already adjusting to that activity, your spot on the coach will also have an environmental factor to switching your mind to the routine activity. This can help to your advantage as you plan a certain time of day you will devote solely to working on your Avatarhood, whatever it may look like to you. If you are starting a business for a service to help others, 6pm to 8pm might look like a guaranteed scheduled time to work on it if you also have a full-time job. At first, it will seem difficult, though after forcing yourself to do so, you will find that it becomes second nature and will automatically float to your office when it is time.

Forcing yourself, in the beginning, will be a huge factor in perfecting your stability. It is a skill that will hold up your foundation once you become more adjusted to doing it. Imagine you had a long day at work. Customers yelled at you, your boss made you stay late, you are tired. When you come home from that, it's hard to want to go work on your new business. You will feel unmotivated. By practicing doing the small things, you will find that it will be easier to pull out the why you have to make your business, and just do it anyways. This is called volition, and it is the opposite of motivation. Volition is using pure willpower to do something instead of engaging with something because you feel like doing it.

If Sokka had volition when he was stuck in the hole, then he may not have made that promise or would have kept it once he was out. Sokka would have been meat-free for the rest of the series. Like that, if you are on a diet and are hungry and see you have a choice of pizza or a salad- you know which one you should choose. That's all the information you need for the volition choice. No matter what you pass through, take the correct choice instead of taking an easy way or shortcut.

<u>Accountability</u>

Foundations must be held accountable. When laying bricks, the cement holds them in place to make sure they hold up the building. In earth bending, the rock will not move unless the bender is there moving it. Having a system to hold you accountable for your goal will keep the foundation in place.

Systems can look like one of the two ways or a combination of both. Choosing the best one to motivate you to stay on top of your goals is essential. We have characters in the series who are held accountable for their own behavior, their mission, and their role in life. This has been seen with Zuko's character arc, Aang defeating the Fire Lord and Korra to stay neutral when the Water Tribe Civil War started. Each has different ways to hold them to be their best.

The first system is seen the most within the series, which is human accountability. This could be a single person holding you accountable or an entire group holding you accountable. Aang had his friends hold him accountable for learning the element to defeat the Fire Lord. That same group held Zuko accountable to be good once he joined the group. Connect with someone who is willing to hold you accountable to your journey daily. If you plan to work on your Avatar hood at a certain time every day, then, set up a system to send them a picture or text stating that you are doing it at that time. Have check-in calls with each other where you talk about your progress. Be as open and vulnerable as you can be with them. This partnership will most likely include their goals as well, be there for them and help them stay accountable to their own goals.

When forming a group, make sure it is completely on the table what you are looking for from them. When in a group, it's not recommended to have more than 4-5 people in it. The bigger the group is, the more people have to share their own goals and give feedback. Meetings will take longer and harder to do daily at the same time. You could change the group dynamic a little by having different people keep you accountable for different parts of your life. One person is supposed to make sure you go to the gym while another one is there to make sure you work on your career. Find the best system for you when working with people.

The second system you could make is a reward and consequence system. This system is like the reward-wanted posters for The Runaway. If you complete the task, you get the reward. In that case, if you turn in The Runaway, you get the reward money. On your journey, there will be milestones you will come across that can be treated as such. For instance, if weight loss is part of your overall goal, once you lose a certain amount of weight, then, you can reward yourself by getting a new pair of shoes or other workout clothing. Something that won't contradict the goal you just achieved. Or in the case that you missed the gym when you were supposed to, you could have to donate $50 to a charity you do not like. Both ways will motivate you to achieve the goal and stay accountable to the process to reach that goal.

This system can be a bit tricky as it will be hard to keep yourself accountable to it. For instance, if you say you will purchase a new fitness watch once you lose 25 lbs but don't hit your goal, you could still get the watch anyways. It's a matter of your discipline to not buy the watch when the goal is not met. Or if you said you would donate

$100 to the political campaign of your opposing views if you miss a day at the gym and decide after missing that you are not going to go through with that promise. It is critical that you go through exactly as you said the reward/consequence would be. If you ease up on it even a little, you will take it less seriously and lose its benefits immediately.

There is a way to help reinforce the integrity of the second system to work more flawlessly. Add an accountability partner to the mix. If you miss a day at the gym, then, your partner will contact you and hold you accountable for the consequence you agreed on. You could even take it a step further and have to send them the money to make sure you still go through with it and they will spend it on the agreed prospect. The sure way to keep your foundation solid and accounted for is the help of others to call you out when you do not go through with your word.

Continue To Relook At The Foundation

Work of the foundation is never done. It is important to keep a constant look at it for improvements. Looking for the cracks in the foundation that are slowing you down can be the difference between your foundation breaking and holding strong. If you let a crack continue to grow, it will eventually let in unwanted substances or worse of all let parts or all of your foundation fall.

The way you will evaluate your foundation is as simple as taking ten minutes at the beginning of every week. In these ten minutes, you will answer two questions. The first question will be "What did I do this past week?" Take this question as extensive as you can by looking at your actions and what rewards they produced. Then you will ask the second question, "What can I do better to go forward?" This is the part where you will pick out the flaws in your week and plan on making them better. Take this time to really plan on what needs to be improved and how you will do this.

.   When going through these weekly meetings, it is recommended to write them down on paper. Leave it as a physical log that you can go back to whenever you need it. Maybe you can find a pattern of something that you did not notice before. These logs will let you look back if you get stuck. Your ability to see the results of the previous weeks will enable you to know what a fresh week has for you. So much information come and go in a single week that it is impossible to remember each detail that happens. Letting the experience out onto paper, better yet a journal can give you a place to consult when you feel you have reached a dead end.

Leaving The Comfort Zone

Your journey will be full of opportunities to go places you've never been before. Many of these opportunities are missed by people who are anxious, doubtful, and scared. Those are the flight responses to keep you in the comfort zone. Part of earth bending is initiating the fight response to help leave the comfort zone.

Leaving the comfort zone is the difference between people being able to move boulders vs moving pebbles. Or in this case, people becoming successful with their goals vs people who never reach their goals and give up. It takes strenuous work to be able to move a boulder by yourself. Work that will make your body tense up and go under intense pressure to keep it up. If someone refuses to go through the muscle-building work to be able to move a boulder, they will never move past moving some pebbles. As they say, no pain no gain.

In your journey, the only boulder you will be moving is your goals. Unless you are striving to become extremely fit and strong to do a strongman competition, there is no need to actually go out and move a physical boulder around. Instead, you will have to find what the tasks are that are hard for you to accomplish your goal. You can make a list if you want, make yourself aware of traits, such as public speaking, you need to accomplish. In the end, that won't make doing the tasks any easier. You will still be in the position you were before, instead faced with everything you have to force yourself to do.

Getting yourself ready to do such tasks will start small. Look at the public speaking scenario. Like when Sokka gave his war speech in the episodes of *Day of Dark Sun*, it is hard to go out in front of a crowd, or online, or anywhere where you are speaking about your own knowledge and opinions to people. While there are many tactics to help with public speaking and to get better at it, we are looking at one aspect in general of the whole ordeal- actually doing something that terrifies you. This is ultimately going out of your comfort zone. To achieve getting to a point where we can do such a task as leaving the comfort zone, we need to practice.

Practicing this act can be done in small segments in your everyday life. For instance, when you take your shower for the day, instead of having the normal warm shower, take a cold shower. Start off with baby steps. First, just turn it too cold for a few seconds during your shower. Then each day increase the time you have it be cold until it is the entire length of your normal shower time. Do this continually. This technique has a few different benefits to it, which we will cover in a later element. The benefit, for now, is doing something uncomfortable on purpose. From there, carry on doing other uncomfortable situations to adjust your body to do the uncomfortable things instead of initiating the flight response. This can be seen in other parts of your life as you may force yourself to try something new when you eat out, work out in a more intense manner, or even force yourself to talk to a stranger one-on-one.

To take a step further out of the comfort zone, put yourself in situations where you go against the social norm. This is more than just making a fashion statement at work or speaking your controversial opinion. This can be done in any public setting at any time, for instance, a check out at a store. When in line, lay down on the ground for 30 seconds. Then resume as if nothing happened. If people point out what you did, act like it was normal for those to do so. This is not a chance to break the law, but a chance to break the social norms that are programmed into your mind. Think of Toph and how she presents herself. Her parents raised her to give in to her disability, to be polite, and to be gentle. She broke from that and became the best earth bender in the world, participating in earthbending fighting matches. To achieve who you want to be, you will have to go against the comfort zone those around you have helped you create. You will have to be Toph and break some rules!

Environment

When we think of Earth, we consider the environment Mother Nature gives to us. The green forests, vast mountains, expanding valleys, colorful flowers, and much more. When we take ourselves away from nature and into society, we find ourselves surrounded by screens, constant news of political tension, and the comfort of closed doors in our homes. This section is not to tell you to only live out in nature away from society, this is here to teach you the way to manipulate the environment to work for you. An earth bender needs rocks to be able to bend. The best place for them to do so will be outside surrounded by their element.

In your own life, your environment must help support your own situation. If your secret tunnel is not made of the right material, you will never make it to your Omashu. Take into consideration the exposure you have to tragic news, addicting social media, and clutter. Your environment will shape the path you take. Without necessary material and space, you will find yourself failing to leave the concerns over everyday anxiety, anger, tiredness, and depression. These emotions are experienced by most people and with the rise of consumption of media, we see skyrocketing statistics of these emotions turning into mental health issues.

Look at your environment in sections of your life. If certain rooms in your life are set up for specific tasks, it is a lot easier to jump into what needs to get done at the point of entry. For instance, the bedroom is for sleeping while the kitchen is for cooking and eating. When it is not possible to have separate rooms for everything, create zones. For instance, you only have access to a room for your bedroom, have half for sleeping and the other half with your desk for work. Then once you step into that zone you will dedicate yourself to the task at hand.

Within these rooms, consider the organization. A cluttered room will provide a cluttered mind as you fixate on the stuff laid about and in piles. You may find yourself looking through it instead of focusing on the task at hand. Think of when you need to do dishes, but you see that you could pick up the living room instead or do laundry that isn't a full load yet. Essentially, distracting yourself with other tasks that are not a priority. This becomes us when everything around us is out of line, we find other things to do instead of the immediate priority.

One of the biggest distractions people face today is the media and content that is found on screens. It could be a phone, TV, or computer. The amount of science that goes into hooking people into spending hours on these screens has succeeded. Many choose to waste a few hours on Facebook instead of working on the book they have been thinking about for years. While you do not have to give up the luxury of watching your favorite shows or sharing funny cat pictures on the internet, there is a limit you must commit to. Your environment can change, just as nature is always changing. Solutions for resisting the pitfalls of social media and the likes can be found in removing them from your work zones. Turn it off, leave it in a different room, leave it upside down or give it to someone to watch. Remove the technology that you can when it is time to sit down and dig your secret tunnel. If your tunnel involves a computer to do work, block websites that are not part of your work, such as Facebook or Instagram. Limit the access you have to it. Follow through with any solution you give.

When the time comes to dabble in your social media, keep aware of the content you are taking in. Even when watching the news on TV, be aware of the content. If you surround yourself with the constant tragic talk of a news channel it will overtake you. You can find that this happens with other forms of entertainment such as music and reading. If you consume depressing material, you will naturally feel that way most of the time.

The action to take after becoming aware of your environment is to find alternatives. Find music and literature that aren't always depressing, but some that give you more positive feelings. Limit the amount of negative news you bring in to the minimum of just being aware of what's going on. Getting tied up in world affairs too much can cause you to steer away from your Omashu. Unless it directly affects what you want to achieve, keep the exposure down to a minimum.

<u>Bringing These All Together</u>

Once you have worked through the above segments, it will be time to see them work together. The goal is to find a balance to intertwine these to cement your foundation to be strong. Plan your day ahead of time to make sure each one is touched on in the way it needs to. Give your full attention to the parts that need more help. Looking back and forward will not only help you with your goals but also with seeing these all work together. You may find that you missed a habit that you need to discard, but changing it will cause an adjustment to your environment. For example, you may find you need to stop letting people walk in and talk to you when you are working, so you start to close your door with a do not disturb sign on it.

Do not expect it all to work seamlessly the second you put it all together. If something does not work out, you can always find a solution and change the direction of your secret tunnel. When your foundation starts working to expectations, you will see a change in how often you may have to go through and change aspects of it. Stick to your foundation, but always be open to a better way of doing something. That is how you will improve and become the best Avatar you can be.

The Metal Element

Your foundation created with your Earth bending will create many opportunities for you. The basic plan should be followed, but there is no reason to ignore new opportunities that may increase the potential of your overall goal. Metal is an element of new opportunity. No one before the Last Air bender series could bend it, that we know of. Toph, on the other hand, with her Earth bending mastery, was able to open a new opportunity by manipulating her foundation within the metal. The little bits of earth in metal were hers for the taking because she had mastered her element to the max of its potential. Once she was in a position where moving the metal walls was her only option of escape, she put herself in front of the opportunity to create metal bending. She was so attuned to her own foundation that she could find the bits of Earth within the metal. With her mastery of this, she was able to create a new path by beating the odds of someone being able to move metal, ultimately setting her free so she may be the bender she wants to be instead of hiding it from her parents.

How You Will Know You Are Ready

Knowing that you are ready will take time as you mold your body and mind to respond to the foundation you have built automatically. It will become second nature. While you will still feel a push and pull here and there to go off track, it will be easier to stick your heels in the ground and say no to resistance. Habits can take about three months to form *if you are consistent every day*. Once you miss one day, you are back to zero for that habit. So, have the accountability systems up, journal through your personal growth, be aware of the progress that is happening.

Mastering this element can seem like you are climbing a mountain, and in a sense you are. So many things must be looked at and worked through. You are transforming and letting go of how your life has been for years if not your entire life. To help stay on track, here is a checklist to measure where you are. Each item should be scored on a 1-10 rating. 1 is the lowest indicating that you have nothing and have only read the section. 10 will be the highest and means you are confident in the work you have done in that section and see no more need to improve it. Add up the scores at the end and look at your overall score. Think of it as a letter grade in school, 90-100 is an A, 80-89 is a B, 70-79 is a C, 60-69 is a D and everything below that is an F. The goal here is to reach for an A. While other scores are considered passing, they don't indicate mastery. You could move on in the average level grades such as B and C, though be aware there is a possibility for fatal cracks in your foundation. Some extra time looking at the lower scores of your checklist will help in the long run.

____ You have journaled and are fully aware of the traits and
        habits you have discarded.
____You have journaled and have a full, clear vision of your
Omashu
____You have mapped out the Secret Tunnel to get to your
Omashu
____ You have journaled through and established clear and
effective Ground Rules
____ You have created an effective morning/ daily routine to
        achieve your Omashu.
____ You have a near-flawless accountability system that you are
keeping too.

_____ You have established when as well as followed through with evaluating your foundation.

_____ You have embraced becoming uncomfortable and leaving your comfort zone

_____ You have evaluated and made changes to your environment.

_____You feel confident in how these all work together.

_____ Overall score

After you have your score, take a moment to reflect on what you have accomplished so far. Getting to a point where you can say you've mastered an element is no small feat. Going forward will bring you much closer to becoming a fully realized Avatar.

The Lava Element

Lava bending is a rare element that will represent exceptional advancement to us. You will strive to be the best you can in your journey, and the way you do that is by finding a way to get an edge on the competition. The root will always be important as you go through your life, being able to fall back into a for sure backing such as your foundation. Lava is what happens when you take a chance once you have mastered your element. Bolin discovered he was a lava bender when he tried his last efforts, putting himself as a sacrifice to protect Tenzin and his siblings from the oncoming lava. He used his mastery of the element and put himself forward on an attempt he did not know he could do, though he was willing to sacrifice himself to succeed. This brought the ultimate response as he was able to stop the lava from killing them all. When you are able to bend lava, you will be using your mastered foundation to rise above all those around you in a fashion that will surprise everyone. It will be a situation only you could have handled in that way.

Fire

Your next step in the journey of Avatarhood will be to master Fire. This element has a high-powered feeling to it. Like the element itself, you will feel a warm inspired spark that will grow over time. You will essentially, as Zuko put it, "rise with the sun". This element is not for the faint of heart.

Fire carries the energy that you will need in your journey. Think of the energy the sun brings with it as it rises each morning. It gives you energy for the day, nutrients to grow your food, warmth to carry on. Mastering this power will drive the days ahead as you work towards your Omashu. Your desires in life will roar like a raging fire as you implement your training into your daily life. The willpower to reach the top will come naturally.

Before going on, it is important to understand this element in a positive, respectable, good-natured light. Think of when the dragons taught Aang and Zuko the beauty of fire in the episode *The Firebending Masters*, there was no hatred and anger in it. It was beauty and life that they found in it. Even when Aang was holding the little amount of fire he was given to present to the masters, he said "It's like a little heartbeat" to which the Sun Warrior Chief summed it up as "Fire is life, not just destruction." Take these words into consideration as you work through this element. This element is not about powering through like a tyrant, ultimately dominating anything you do. This element is meant to bring inspiration, life, and energy into yourself to accomplish your dreams.

While Earth held the main idea of foundation in your journey, Fire will hold the notion of energy. Energy is the strength and vitality used to sustain your physical or mental activity. While you will always have your foundation to fall back on, it is important to maintain the fuel, momentum, and power needed to follow through with your journey. This will go beyond the aspects of getting enough sleep, eating healthy, exercise and consumption of caffeine. You will be mastering the tricks to combat the mind when it tries to bring you down, instead of turning it into burning energy that will achieve anything you put your mind to.

Characteristics of a Fire Bender

Before you have your first lesson on the element of fire, it is important to see what makes a fire bender. Many characters can be claimed as firebenders, though not all of them should be idolized as such. During the Hundred Year War, we saw strong and powerful benders such as Zhao, Azula, and Ozai. These characters lost themselves in their use of the element and ultimately fell into the failure of their goals. Characters that showed admirable understanding of the elements include Uncle Iroh, Mako, General Iroh, Rangi, Avatar Roku, and even Zuko. Zuko's journey shows the growth that a firebender can have once he grasps onto the true power of fire.

The characteristics of these firebenders range from physical to mental strength. We see powerful punches and kicks as they dance around in their formations. We see finely tuned focus on their desired target. The grasp they have on their own personal rules. The knowledge they possess in all circumstances. There is no getting past the threat of achievement these benders are capable of.

Seeing a firebender is much more than a personal inner discipline, they have a culture full of it. They are all tied to the concept of honor. The idea is that their accomplishments and failures reflect those of their nation, ruling poor outcomes to be shameful. There will be more on how this concept will affect you later on, for now, it is important to be aware of the high importance it is in the culture. We saw Zuko for nearly two seasons chase the Avatar for the sheer hope of being recognized as the worthy prince he was to his father and people. In the Kyoshi novels, we saw Hei-Ran cut her own hair off as a sign of dishonor for the crimes that she had once committed. Multiple times, we saw Agni-kias happen as a duel for honor. Honor should not be seen as a hindrance as it may come off at times, instead, we will learn how to use it to uplift all those around us.

The emotional control of firebenders will also play a part in your journey. There are two sides of the spectrum that we will look at, one where we see many hotheaded benders lose their temper and the ones that know how to breathe and walk away. The temper of a firebender has played many roles in this world, as we watched Zhao lose his control, Zuko making rash decisions, and Mako creating unneeded tension. Though we have also seen it being controlled as Iroh patiently guided Zuko to a path better suited for him.

As you tread through these upcoming lessons in the art of fire bending, remember the intentions of traits from characters. If you rush through with poor intentions you will get burned. Think of Aang when he was learning fire bending with Jeong Jeong, he rushed through the training and ended up burning Katara. Fire can be used to help and grow those around us rather than take them down, trust in the process of those who have truly mastered it.

Uncle Iroh's Wisdom

"It is best to admit mistakes when they occur, and to seek to restore honor."

The Avatar is human and will make mistakes. This is where you will have to put pride and embarrassment aside and come clean when you mess up. This will build honesty with yourself and with others. To restore your honor is to keep your honesty true and your character and a path of growth and righteousness.

<u>Your Flame</u>

Desire can range from a simple want to a burning sensation where you must do everything in your power to get something. Within your flame of energy, you will have a mixture of things that will build it up. Your desire is the first component in building a bright bountiful flame that will flicker on for years to come. This will be more than simply wanting something really bad. In the end, when you do not have enough energy to continue feeding that desire, it will fade away. You will need to build it up to burn even through the roughest of storms you will encounter.

Think of a scale of different colors of fire. From lowest temperature to highest temperature the scale goes red, orange, white, and then blue. Anything lower than red is non-existent on the flame scale while you cannot get anyone hotter than blue. Going off of this, you will see how much desire you truly have for something. For instance, let's take losing weight as an example. In this example, let's say that a person wants to lose weight for aesthetic purposes, to look better in clothing. They also had a talk with their doctor that their cholesterol has gone up again. They will start off their journey not on the blue flame, even if they feel inspired. Instead, they will most likely be on the lower end of the orange flame. There is a drive that will be bright at first, but they will watch it burn out.

They could try and feed their flame with a challenge, such as a marathon, though that will not be enough to bring them fully into the white flame. A coach or trainer could help feed the flame, to help it burn brighter. But what happens when they are not there? Your flame will get dimmer with less material to burn. Your motivation and energy will fall trap of excuses and tomorrow.

What you will need is an everlasting material to feed you the strength to push forward. The best source will be to find your ultimate "why" for wanting something. A reason to remind yourself of the potentially painful reason you need to accomplish something. This part of your journey will involve looking deep into the motives of your fears, anxieties, and other drives in life. To begin, you will have to get your journal ready and the intention of uncovering any emotion and experience that relates to the goal at hand.

Taking the weight loss example, the first question will be "Why do I want to lose weight?" These are your initial why's. Now, go deeper into why you want each one of those reasons. You may start with "Why do I want to look better in clothing?" where you can expand into how you have never been able to wear a two-piece swimsuit. Expanding more into it might go like this-:

-"Why have I never been able to wear this two-piece swimsuit?"- Because I feel people will judge me and say I shouldn't wear that.
-"Why do I fear that will happen?"- Because I've heard people body shame someone before at a public pool on how they are too fat to wear the two-piece.
- "Why do I care about what those people think?"- Because I was bullied in school for my looks, they called me names, and I cried in the bathroom at the school dance.

Go deep into it. Talk about the hard times and how it is affecting you now. These are the experiences that shape everyone- good or bad there is always a time you can pinpoint that shaped an aspect of yourself. You must acknowledge these instances to be able to work past them. In gastric bypass surgery, Doctors will not operate on you unless you lose x-amount of weight, see counseling, and can prove you can keep up a lifestyle to sustain the new projected body. It is never about just eating less and moving more, it is about why you got in that place in the first place. Going off of this, continuing the journal may look something like this:

- "Why should I stop caring about what they think?" because this trauma has pushed me to binge eating when I am upset, and now, whenever I start to feel upset, I go to eat right away.

At this point in the journal, the main root of the cause is being exposed. The trauma has surfaced and the result of it as well has ultimately created the thing that wants to be changed. This is not a journey to point at and blame others for your misfortune. Think of Azula, how after her friends Mai and Ty Lee chose to defy her in the episode *The Boiling Rock Part 2,* she started to descend into madness banishing everyone. She blamed everyone for all of her misfortune instead of stepping back and considering what different behavior she could have done to work through everything. This is not saying you are in the wrong, this is saying that once you start blaming everyone, you become blind to real solutions.

The next step will be discovering the real solution to the problem. In this case, it could be a number of options that could include improving your relationship with your body or working on your dependence on what others think. Really explore the options as well as choose more than one if you wish. Sometimes go through the other whys for a problem before committing to something. In this case, the reason for the cholesterol going up can be explored.

- "Why is my cholesterol going up significantly?" - Because it is common in my family history as well as other health issues.
- "Why does my family's health history concern me?" - I lost one parent when I was a small child to a sudden heart attack.
- "Why does that scare me?"- That could happen to me and abandon my own family.

The ultimate why will show you the life you don't want to live or be responsible for. It is more than just knowing something would be bad. It will be the worst thing you could think of if you don't change. This will be the ultimate drive to reach your goals. If you remind yourself of the why when you start to lose desire, look at what you found to be your why.

From there, the person might find that the route of creating a new relationship with their body may be the right path for them to take. Be detailed in the path you want. Think of Zuko's in the beginning of the series, he wanted to capture and bring the Avatar to his father so that his father would recognize him as his honorable son, allow him to be home, and reclaim his birthright to being the heir of the throne. Know the reason, the outcome, and how to get it. When the path is as clear to you as it was at the time to Zuko, you will have the motivation like he did as he sailed the seas searching for years for a person no one had seen in a hundred years, without for once giving up hope.

Once you have gone through the process of finding your "why," it is time to reevaluate your desire on the flame scale again. The goal is to dig deep enough to feel the burning desire of blue. The only way you will ever reach that is if you add the right fuel to the mix. Become vulnerable and accept the true reasons you desire an outcome.

<u>Feeding Your Flame</u>

While you may be feeding your flame with your "whys" from the desire section, there is more to feeding your flame. Fire is more than just one chemical, there are multiple in this chemical reaction. The phenomenal part of it is it's not always the same fuel, the basic equation to create fire is heat + oxygen + a fuel = fire. It is the same with your own flame. Think of desire as your heat. Now, we will focus on your fuel. Your fuel doesn't have to be this huge deep philosophical journey you go on. It is mainly the content and other sources you will consume to feed your flame.

There are a number of sources you can turn to for this, in the end, it will be a matter of preference. You may indulge in nonfiction books on certain topics such as mindset, motivation, relationships, and so on. Influencers who talk about fitness, business, or life in general. Podcasts diving into topics of interest and growth. Conversations with certain people on their outlooks on life matters. Your fuel will be what will help reinspire you when you need it. Think of it as throwing another log on the fire. If you feel your flame is getting weaker, throw something in there to help keep it going. Do not think of this as motivation, instead, stick with inspiration- a reason to approach something in a certain way.

In the series, we see less approach to the media intake, beyond the fact some may have felt inspired to help the Civil War efforts with the Nuttuk movers. Instead, we see Zuko consulting his uncle, Iroh, Avatars consulting past lives, stories, and tales being told of past events such as the hundred years of war. There are numerous different ways you can find your fuel. You may find it in nature, other hobbies, and sitting in silence. The idea is to find what fuels your fire best. What helps ignite that flame to burn brighter than ever before.

Going a step further in feeding your flame will be the basics of self-care. These everyday treatments of sleep, food, hydration, and movement are designed to help the mind in day-to-day function. If your body is not prepared for the inspiration, it will approach everything impaired and distraught. Watching Aang struggle with not sleeping before the invasion is just one example of what can start happening.

Consider as well as experiment with the amount of sleep you function best with. There is the recommended 7-9 hours, where you might find 7 is enough and anymore makes you groggy. On the other hand, you may find you function better at the latter side of the recommendation. Do the same with all aspects of decent self-care. Just because people say vegetables such as broccoli and brussel sprouts are good for you does not mean your body is good at digesting them. Your body uses the most energy to digest food, if you are having trouble digesting it you may feel tired and bloated, leading to you not having the energy to want to go about your day the way you intended it. Find what works for you the best, in the end, no one can argue to eat something that makes you less effective in your journey.

Movement is not a disguise for exercise. While you can choose to implement running, strength training, or any other vigorous exercise you want that you find your body likes, it doesn't have to be as extreme as that. Take for example, a simple walk once or twice a day. The idea is to just make your body move. Science has shown that movement can increase your brain activity and efficiency by increasing the amount of oxygen in brain cells and promoting the production of new cells. There is also the option of getting up to walk around the house a little after being sedentary after an hour. The body was never meant to not move for long periods of time, to optimize it, look for reasons to move throughout the day. You may even find that your focus, problem solving and ideas skyrocket from doing so!

Fire benders are very diligent in their work and tend to be punctual with what needs to be done. Iroh many times suggests to Zuko to rest, eat, drink tea, and even go for a walk to clear his head. Each one with the intent to help clear Zuko's mind and get him to see something more clearly than rushing in with his raw emotion. Take the time to listen to the body and act on what it needs. Frustration is a hindrance to energy which we will find later in this element. Do what you can to move past it and be inspired by new outlooks and feelings.

<u>Willpower</u>

The third part of the fire equation is volition, or in other words, willpower. Volition will be the oxygen in the fire equation. You may have fuel and heat, but unless the oxygen has access to the source there will be no fire. Think of it like putting a lid on top of your fire, preventing any more air from getting in, the fire will die. Your own fire will die if you do not master volition.

Before we dig deep into what successful volition looks like, it is important to note that it is not motivation. Motivation is powered by emotion. You do things on a basis if you feel like it rather than doing so anyways. Mako shows motivation at its best and worst in season two of The Legend of Korra. When Mako and Korra were fighting in the police station, Mako felt the emotion needed to push through ending their relationship. His anger in the situation fueled his decision to end the relationship at that moment. Later in the season, we see the two "back together" due to Korra losing part of her memory and not remembering they broke up. Once it was clear that she thought he was still her boyfriend, Mako hesitated and said nothing. He knew he should tell her, especially since his current girlfriend, Asami, was there. Instead, his emotion told him to fear hurting Korra again, which led Mako to listen to that logic and not say anything. Motivation is entirely emotion-driven, it will deter you from what you need to do to achieve your desired outcome. In Mako's case, it was to keep Asami.

In your life, you may experience this by saying you will wake up early and go to the gym. By the time the alarm goes off, the motivation is gone and your tired state wins as it hits the snooze button. You may even find yourself trying to find the motivation to get up and put the dishes away but talk yourself into doing it tomorrow because you are already too comfy on the couch. Motivation can come in handy when it sparks at the right moment, but sparks can go out if left on their own.

If volition took place, you would be up and at the gym when the alarm goes off and putting away dishes even if you just sat down to watch TV. Mako would have gone through and hurt Korra by breaking up with her once again. While he did not want to hurt her again, it was the move that had to happen for his current relationship. The concept of volition will never run out, it is a matter of doing something whether you want to or not. Motivation, though, runs out quickly. The second you have a new emotion in the mix, motivation vanishes. It keeps you from completing tasks you need to do. To achieve results, you need to let go of motivation as a whole.

After the Day of Black Sun, we saw Zuko perform marvelous volition. He knew his new path, to teach the Avatar fire bending to take down his father. While a scary path that involved having to change the minds of people, he has been hunting for the past year, he never gave up. Even when joining the group, he went out of his way to go on separate journeys with individual members of the team to prove his loyalty to them.

In your training, you are not expected to put your life in danger to convince someone you have changed. Instead, you will start small on your journey to mastering volition. Remember the cold shower from your earth training? Here we will expand on the benefits of it. Not only will it train you to go outside your comfort zone, but it will train you to continually do it while you don't want to, not that you wanted to in the first place. The idea is to do it every day to train your mind to do a small thing you know you don't want to do. Ignore the feeling of dread or frustration and do it anyway.

Find more ways to train this into you. The key is to find something you want to be a habit. Making your bed in the morning could be an excellent one to do. Nothing bad will happen if you don't make your bed, you will still live. It takes extra time in the morning and you will just get into it anyways at the end of the day. The perfect excuse to do something anyways and build up the volition. As soon as you wake up in the morning, make the bed every morning. Even if you are running late, take a few moments to accomplish this. It will not only be a practice, it will also set the day up with a win.

There are many habits you could use for this. Maybe it will be washing a dish once you are done with it instead of letting it sit there, putting away laundry as soon as the dryer is done, taking the trash out before it is spilling over. There are a number of small things you could use in your training. Find the daily habits you want to implement into your life and add them one at a time. Overloading this will have an opposite effect and will burn you out.

Once you have a grasp on the small things, see how much easier the bigger things will go. At the end, big accomplishments are a bunch of small accomplishments, making it more important that you follow through with each one. Push yourself to do things when you think about not wanting to. Send the email right now instead of later. Clean your room now instead of right before you have company over. Go to the gym now instead of saying you'll go tomorrow. Meal prep when you say you will. There is no secret to success, it is just a matter of letting motivation go and inviting volition in.

<u>Sacrifice</u>

The idea of sacrificing things can be, overwhelming enough for you to really evaluate if you want to do something. Choosing to let something go may be one of the hardest things to do. Our concept of this won't go as far as some sacrifices in the series such as Avatar Roku giving his life to save the island he lives on, Firelord Sozin sacrificing Roku to start a war, Ozai sacrificing his son's honor for his own example, or Ursa sacrificing her life with her family to protect Zuko and make Ozai Fire Lord. As you can see, fire benders are not strangers to big sacrifices in their lives. You on the other hand will be tackling this in a different manner.

When you only have so much time in a day, it's hard to make sure you can get everything done that you want to get done. It is harder when you start to feel tired towards the end of the day when you may have time to work on your Secret Tunnel. This is where you need to find out what to sacrifice. You may sacrifice sleeping late in the morning so that you may work on your Secret Tunnel before the rest of your day. Or you could wake up earlier to exercise to give yourself some extra energy for the day or to pack a healthy lunch.

During your lunch break, you may sacrifice half of it to make a few calls concerning your Secret Tunnel. A step further you may eat a quick snack and work through the lunch to go home early to get extra time on something that needs to get done. There may be an event or party you miss here or there due to a pressing matter that could help you get to your Omashu sooner. The possibilities are endless when it comes to cutting something out to get things done at the moment with the energy you do have. This doesn't mean you have to stop seeing people and enjoying your breaks at your 9 to 5. This is something to consider when you are striving to become the best Avatar you can be.

If you throw your life slightly out of balance, once you complete what you are focusing on during that time, that aspect will grow and bear fruit to the other areas of your life. For instance, your focus on a business you are starting up while distancing yourself from gatherings and events for a while, also spending half the time with your family as usual. Once the time gap is done and you resume with the parts that were cut short, everything will have to shift for the better in a sense. If you focus on extra time on the business, then it will generate more money. With the increase in income, you can afford to take your family on a nice vacation or provide more of the necessities and luxuries.

Consider the Avatar when they travel the world to learn all four elements. They sacrifice years of their life to just train. Once they return to their home, they are not only better in their bending, but can provide better for their family, friends, nation, and the world. Taking selected amounts of time to work on one thing will dramatically speed it up faster than if you try and juggle everything at once.

It is easier said than done, as you probably have a busy life with work, bills, family, friends, and other obligations. Talk with those around you to help you set up a time to be able to use the life out of balance technique. Find your support system and a plan. This doesn't have to be for years, it could be a week or two. Sacrificing that chunk of time to focus strictly on one thing will go a long way. The longer may help in the end getting your Omashu here quicker, but it isn't always a luxury. When you do get the chance to do this, make a full plan with goals before it. This could even be a week of just working on your own personal transformation as long as you are clear with those who are going to help you or see less of you during it.

Never sacrifice this time without a plan. When a business goes through a time like this, they call it a Push. They set a time for this, it could be a week or two. They plan with employees on their goals for each day, being honest with each other that they may be pushing home life aside for the time, making sure they communicate with their families that it will only be for the planned time. The time is never wasted, instead, they work to push each other farther than they were before, making their normal quotas in a workday naturally go up since they trained themselves to see they can accomplish even higher numbers.

Keeping all of this in mind, find time to implement this into your life, even if it's only the weekends for a month. While it's not an everyday thing, finding the imbalances will bring you closer to your ultimate balanced life where you have reached your Avatar potential.

Aim Before You Shoot Your Flame

Once you have balanced your equation for fire, it will be time to start using that new energy. How you use your energy will currently be the focus. In the sections before this, we have talked about how to get the energy needed. Having the energy will not magically make what you want to happen. Think of Zhao in the episode *The Deserter* as he aimlessly shot his fire at Aang only to end up burning his own ship. Taking the time to direct towards the right path will help avoid the destruction of your own goals.

There has been much planning already, and by now you should know that it will be the key to your success. Take into consideration your purpose of action before you start putting your energy towards something. The action you are about to take may not actually require as much energy as you thought or any at all. Zuko, at the end of book one, attempted to kidnap Aang and fled into the cold icy, and snowy desert the North Pole is. He put all his energy into getting into the snowy fortress and grabbing Aang. There was no outlook on the entire picture, once he escaped the city into the snowy wasteland there was nowhere to go. If it weren't for Team Avatar finding him and Aang insisting they take him with them for safety, he would have died out there without accomplishing his goal of restoring his honor and returning home.

Zuko found it more successful during the times that he stopped and focused on what he needed to do. Standing up to his father was one way. Zuko only entered his father's chamber to tell him the truth during the solar eclipse that blocks their fire bending. By doing this, he has planned to have less conflict with him and leave before his father could do anything about it. Instead of trying to take the whole matter into his own hands to take down his father, he took the basic steps and left for more help. If Zuko had stayed to duel his father, his escape would have been eliminated. He understood the power and skill difference between them, which he would not be able to even fully go through with murdering his father. If the old Zuko had faced his father, Zuko would have run into the same problem, except his father would have probably given him more than a burn scar on his eye.

On your journey, take time to learn what is worth your energy. For example, let's say you are trying to build muscle. To build muscle, you need to put it under extreme pressure during exercise to give signals to grow. If you work out too hard too often, you can end up with an opposite effect. The muscle will be damaged too much too often, leaving the body in a constant heal mode instead of being able to switch to the building mode. Or you could see poor results if you don't put any of your energy into the necessary diet you need to build and maintain that kind of muscle mass. To build the body you are aiming for you will need to work out with enough frequency to give your body enough rest between workouts as well as take some of your energy into making sure you are eating adequately enough.

You will need to learn from experience, research, or acquire professional help. Each of these will guide you to the balance that you need to achieve your Omashu. While experience may take longer, it can bring great wisdom over time. Iroh is a great testament to that as we see him pick and choose his battles, no longer taking on every conflict that comes his way. Research is a great method to find the information you wouldn't have known otherwise, like how Zhao learned about the Moon Spirits in Wan Shi Tong's Spirit Library.

Recruiting professional help, such as a coach or teacher, can be beneficial as you will be given the blueprint that they have used to be successful.

Is it possible to use too much energy looking for balance in energy? Of course yes. It is a matter of letting go of fears and anxieties of failure. If you are looking for answers and only get the same information time after time, it is time to start doing it. Even before then, try what you learn as you learn it. Seek the counsel of others to get more insight. But do not do anything because you are afraid of being wrong. Failure is life's greatest teacher. Learning from experience will always be a promising path. Consider Zuko's Agni Kia with his father. Ozia ended the match with a permanent wound to Zuko's face. When we see Zuko fight Zhao to an Agni Kia in the episode *The Southern Air Temple*, we see something different happen. When Zuko is about to claim victory by burning Zhao's face, Zuko gives him mercy by missing his shot on purpose. Zuko had learned the cruel lessons of being burned from the fight, with that he had enough empathy to spare someone else with that hurt and humiliation.

Something to help with this process is to write out everything you need to do. Then circle the top three things. Those are what need your energy right now. Before starting them, determine your expectations of each one. What do you want to achieve and what is the goal? Make sure you are setting a chunk of energy aside for it, but nothing else. There will be more things that will need energy. If you use it all at once, you will need more time to recharge. You will be as drained and useless as a firebender thrown into the cooler at the Boiling Rock.

<u>Redirect Your Flame In Emotion</u>

A trait that needs to be handled now in fire benders is anger. Throughout the series, we see many firebenders being driven by their own emotions. We see Zuko lash out and push those who want to help him away, Zhao using a moment of spite to kill one of the Moon Spirits, Azula's breakdown at the end of the Last Airbender. Once Zuko joins Team Avatar, we see that anger had fueled his bending once he was no longer able to use it. Relying on raw emotion to guide you will lead to your demise. Emotions will cause you to make rash decisions, create spiteful motives in your work, and will come back to blast you in the face. If you are on your journey to becoming the Avatar to get back at someone, reconsider what you really want out of life and return back to this book.

The dragons will be our teachers here, as they taught Zuko a new way to bend fire without his built-up anger and trauma. When we meet the dragons, it is after Firelord Sozin appropriated hunting dragons for a title of being a master. They were thought to be extinct, with the knowledge that Iroh had killed the last one. When Zuko was face to face with them, it could have been justified for the dragons to kill him for revenge. Zuko was part of a family line that led the dragons to be "extinct". The dragons did not take the opportunity to try and deliver payback, instead, they took the opportunity to show Zuko the beauty in firebending that they knew. With that Zuko was able to understand the creatures better, and why his uncle lied about killing the last one.

The story does not mean that you now need to go out of your way to help those that have hurt you, unless that is what you feel you must do. The story is showing that our energy should be put towards helping those and ourselves for the right reasons. The dragons showed

Zuko their knowledge to bring understanding, an impact that would help them return to the public. Strive to help others not have to suffer and bring positive energy into the world.

If you are striving to make money to get back at someone, to show you are better, what good are you impacting the world with? Once you have more money, what will you do then? Will there have been a reaction you were expecting that might not actually happen? Do you have any more purpose for what you were doing? Really consider your motives and what happens when you accomplish those motives.

Take a moment to journal through your emotions and motives within your journey. Some recommended questions are:

Journal Questions
- Why do I want to be successful on this journey?
- What are my reasons?
- Are my reasons tied to proving my self-worth?
- What are the reasons that are positive that I should focus on?
- When do I see myself leading with my emotions?
- Are these emotions tied to a purpose I should be pursuing?
- How can I change the motives to be positive for myself and those around me?

Taking time now and then to evaluate this will keep you on track of fulfillment. Think of a time you have gotten payback on someone. After it happened, did everything go back to being better or was there still emotion left? Were there feelings of being lost? As humans, it is impossible to ignore emotions, what can be done is learn to work with them.

For example, let's say someone was bullied when they were in school. They feel anger from it, they can't even think of the bully without feeling tense and warm. If they decide to do something with that energy, it could lead to multiple different paths. In this example, they choose to become management so they can push people around. Not just people, but the exact bully they had in school that so happens to work in the same office as them. Their anger is funneled into acts of revenge as they abuse telling the bully what to do. Is there a win in that?

Now, instead of taking that route, let's say our person wants to deal with this energy to make good in the world. Instead of striving to ruin someone's life, they may push for starting a program to help stop bullying. Using their energy, they can be able to comfort and listen to those who also suffer from bullying so that they may be able to help them through the experience or even end it for them. This is the power you can unleash if you choose to direct your emotions towards a new path where others thrive and heal.

People and circumstances that may have hurt you in the past won't just disappear from your memory and emotions by doing this, later on, in another element, we will talk about options of healing from these. For now, focus on acknowledging the emotions and choosing to move forward with a different path. If you do this now, then you will avoid the problem that Zuko had when he lost his firebending.

Uncle Iroh's Wisdom

"Power in firebending comes from the breath, not the muscle."

The willpower you will find doesn't happen easily when you just rush through. You get tired and lose focus. Instead, keep an even pace and control your breath. Breathing is what controls your body, if you change it to match the tempo you need then you will feel the strength of willpower. Weak willpower will turn into motivation and die if you are not careful, take your time, and take care of the entire body.

Strengthen Your Mind

Your mind is only as good as you train it to be. With all the new knowledge you have been bringing in and implementing into your life, do you feel it to be too much at times? It can be overwhelming to bring in so much at once and not want to abandon ship. It seems easy to think about playing it cool as you go throughout all of this, though it can prove challenging. It is time to look at helping our minds expand to be able to handle all of this.

Think of Zuko as he is meditating in front of some lit candles at the beginning of the episode *The Kyoshi Warriors*. They are responding evenly with his breath and mind. He is at that moment, in control. When Iroh interrupts to say that he has news which Zuko will not like, Zuko is able to stay cool with that piece of information- even though he knows something is wrong. That is what we are striving for. The part that we are not striving for is what happens when Zuko learns that the news is that they have no idea where the Avatar is. The flames rose with his anger. He becomes flustered and grabs the map, ultimately concluding that they can't know due to the Avatar being a "master of evasive maneuvering." Instead, it's time to strive for keeping that cool and going into situations with an even more open mind to problem-solving.

Meditation can be a method of achieving this, though it is not the only way. Meditation will be covered more in-depth later on in the

Air element as there are numerous other benefits to this practice. For now, let's only focus on the basics of breathing. While you think you may already be a master of breathing since you do it every day, there are studies done which shows that the practice of controlled breathing can change your mindset. Start by sitting with good posture and closing your eyes. Then take a deep breath in for six counts, hold for six counts and let it out for six counts. Repeat this six times. Take this time to focus your mindset as well as your attention on the task at hand.

While this will help you control your breathing and outlook in the moment, there is no long-term control over your emotional state. Do this when you start to feel angry or anxious. Iroh even said that firebending is about the breath when training Zuko. Controlling your breath will give you control over your body and mind to create and use the energy that you want.

To help prepare for times when your mind will be put to the test, practice putting it in problem-solving scenarios. You do not have to go out and create problems to do this. Find simple puzzles you can do to help keep the mind sharp. These could be as simple as sudoku, crosswords, word searches, and other puzzles you can find in activity books. The idea is that you are exercising the brain to do these tasks and to stay calm and focused on them. Don't always go for the easy ones, find something that will help challenge you. Push the mind to have to deal with information it is having trouble processing. That is where the mind will grow.

Strive for Mako as he does detective work. Think of him when he wasn't even a detective but a low-ranking police officer. When the Southern Water Tribe Cultural Center was bombed in the episode *Peacekeepers*, Mako witnessed a culprit in the act. While the guy got away, Mako was able to see enough information to push him to find out who did it. We watched him continually look through books and put pieces together. As his personal investigation on the matter continued, we saw detectives doubt him and pull pranks on him as they would send him in to see Chief Lin Beifong when she was in a meeting. Mako never lost his temper and became flustered so much that he gave up. Mako ended up cracking the case in the end, even if he was then framed by the ones who really did it.

Mako's life prepared him for pressure such as this as he had a history with the Triads and Triple Threats, pro-bending, and his previous adventure with the Avatar. His mind was already brought to the limits and he conquered them. From this, we can see that you can go beyond some puzzles to prepare. Sports that send lots of information to your brain, such as basketball, can help sharpen it. Past events can even help. Life will always throw stuff at you, take what you can to build off of it, and find daily practices to help you continue to prepare for anything.

Handling The Crossroads

At the end of book two in *The Last Airbender*, Iroh speaks to Zuko about how he has reached a crossroads of his own destiny. Zuko could join Azula to capture the Avatar or he could help the Avatar, take down Azula and keep Ba Sing Se free from the Fire Nation. You will come across many instances where you will have to choose a path to follow. It will not always be a linear path to reach your Omashu, you must be ready to choose where to go.

Being decisive can be a tedious objective when you have to evaluate path sides. Some decisions will take more than a few minutes. You may need a few days to a week or so. But only take that time if you really need to. The longer you wait to decide the harder it will be.

Think of a time you were hungry and could not pick between two or more places to get food from. At that moment, you may have been weighing out prices, time, and other factors. Eventually, you come across some pretty good pros for each side and some valid cons for each side. Something that could have been a few minutes to decide may have turned into a whole ordeal where you settle for something that out of the fact you have become too hungry to care about, or someone chose for you.

Going too quickly on a decision can also happen. Zuko didn't have a long time once poised with that decision. He went with the choice that he had been pursuing for years, even though he had recently started the transformation process of letting his desire to capture the Avatar go. With more time he could have gone over what he was accomplishing since he moved to Ba Sing Se, why he started to move on, and every factor that brought him to where he is. Instead, he was led to regret. He felt confusion and anxiety as he had ended up betraying his uncle in the process, getting tied up in a lie that could have revealed him as a fraud, the new realization of how terrible the war really is. He battled with himself until he chose to flee to help the Avatar. A decision that worked out in the end, but could have blown back up in his face if he was captured and made to face treason consequences.

When faced with a big decision, remember your training so far. Use the breathing techniques, seek counsel, and reevaluate your plan. Keeping true to who you are will be a big one as you face these challenges. Let's say you are faced with a choice to pick between two different people to work with. You've gone through pros and cons of both and you still can't decide. If you don't choose soon, then, you risk one backing out or worse, both of them backing out. You could lose your choice. Put them up against your motives, values, and path. The one you feel fits it the best will be your answer. The choice that aligns with your own vision and morals will want to go in the direction you do. While something seems very qualified and may be a better choice may also be something that hinders you. Ozia is the Firelord and determines Zuko's fate while Iroh is just a retired war hero who wants to leave the past behind. It's plain to see why Zuko would want to choose to please his father rather than Iroh in that moment, one has shown to have more power and control over Zuko. Zuko later realized that Iroh was the real father figure that he was looking for in his journey, someone who aligned more with Zuko's desire to be loved and honored.

There is also another tool you have that can help with decisions, journaling. Use your journal to work through everything about a decision. Look into your true feelings about things, your outcomes, fears, questions, and anything related. As it was said before, writing it all down will make it physical and real to you rather than a thought you don't want to face. This will also give you a way to look back on what you were thinking when you made the decision, something that may help when you start to doubt your decision.

The last piece of advice on this is to be confident when you choose. If you go into it with doubt, then your doubt will come true. You will project the outcome onto it. If you are confident in your decision, then you will see the results that you want. Again, return to the journal when you start to second guess yourself. Remind yourself why you were sure this was the right choice. Letting yourself have anxiety and other mixed emotions on a decision that was made will only drain your energy. It will start to put out the fire you've been working on building this whole time.

Uncle Iroh's Wisdom

"You have come to the crossroads of destiny. It's time for you to choose. It's time for you to choose good."

At this moment, Zuko was faced with a hard choice that would officially break him away from trying to please his father. The answer Zuko had at that moment isn't the important part to look at here. Here you need to choose good. Do more than what Zuko did at this moment and choose humanity over your inner desires. You may find that those desires really meant nothing to you in the end. But the fulfillment of doing good is eternal.

The Combustion Element

Combustion bending is a miraculous skill those can be born with. This skill creates what seems to be a third eye on the user. Benders that possess this are highly feared as there is extreme caution when they face off against Combustion Man and P'Li. As soon as these characters see you, they can strike you down with a blast. People with opposing motives to you will seem to be like this. They may find you to be a threat and try to pursue you to go a different direction. It's like they are throwing a rock at the third eye to blind you. If they succeed, they won't be hurt rather, you will and will be powerless to stop them. Be vigilant on your journey. Keep your Omashu in sight, change your secret tunnel to lose these people if you have to. This does not mean not trusting anyone, it means taking into consideration what you are doing as you work with people. Just because you ask for advice and get it from someone does not mean you have to follow it. Be your own judge if the advice will truly benefit you and steer you away from what you actually want.

<u>Using The Flame To Help Others</u>

Earlier, we talked about changing negative motives to becoming positive ones. In a sense, the easiest way to do that is to help others with similar problems. Here we will be diving deeper into that. This is where you will be putting out more action into the world rather than just working on yourself. Think of Avatar Wan wanting to help spirits and humans coexist as well as help Raava gain control over Vaatu again. Zuko agreed to help the South Pole after the Hundred Year War to see the tribe grow into a self-sustaining nation again. Mako's dedication to fight crime on the police force as well as provide some counsel to Prince Wu. Rangi put aside her own moral code to work with the Flying Opera Company to make sure Avatar Kyoshi was safe. Roku shut down Fire Lord Sozin's idea to have the Fire Nation rule the world to keep the world equal, safe, and balanced.

This does not have to start out as big ambitions as many characters have had. This can be making sure you make at least one person's day better each day. This could be holding a door or sending a smile towards a stranger. The idea is to create a wildfire with your own positive energy. Different energies are contagious, going back to when it was discussed about the people around you, those energies that your closest acquaintances have will transfer to you whether you want it or not. Like a cold, once the germs are given a pathway to you, then you will become sick. In this case, we want to reverse the idea of negative energy being spread and create more positive energy.

When Wan tried to enter the Spirit Oasis, he was giving energy that he should only benefit, there was no intention of helping the spirits. The negative attitude of Aye-aye towards humans transferred onto Wan when they interacted, making Wan rasher in his attempts to enter. Later, when Wan found Mula, the catdeer stuck in a trap, he used positive energy to save its life rather than save his own by eating her. The energy traveled through Mula onto the spirits as they were overjoyed that Wan would do such a thing. In a sense, he restored their hope in humanity.

Even on a bad day, don't share the negative energy you might be dealing with. Choose to spread joy instead. Holding a door with a smile can change the whole trajectory of someone's day. If someone scowled at them and didn't hold the door, the energy of the negative interaction can then transfer to the victim in this case and then cause that person to potentially snap at someone or ignore a plea for help. Consequently, that can start a wildfire of negativity as each person thrusts that energy onto the next people they see. It's almost like dominos are falling towards a ticking time bomb.

Strive to make a difference in the world by positively affecting one person a day to create a new chain of positive energy. If person 1 holds the door and smiles at person 2, then person 2 can later do the same to someone else. Person 2 may even end up saying hi to a lonely person 3 who then goes out of their way to help a person 4 that will impress person 5 and lead to person 5 to then give person 6 a raise because they just so happen to have positive energy when person 6 asks. From there, person 6 can then transfer the energy and so on. A wildfire of positive energy races towards end goals of success and happiness to others around you. In the end, making a true difference in the world as others are affected by your one act of kindness.

It isn't always easy to do the good thing. At times you just want to get inside the building and not worry about who is around you. There are times you may feel pressured to ignore the good thing because you may miss something you were on your way to. It's natural to feel the resistance as the right thing battles with your own desires.

When Zuko rescued Appa by setting him free at Lake Laogai, Aang was able to then reunite with him and felt more positive energy towards ending the war. Later on, the positive energy that was still with Appa led to friendly interactions with Zuko that helped Aang connect with his own positive energy and learn from Zuko. A domino effect helped stir them in the right direction to then focus and end the war.

From this, we can learn that even when we don't want to release the positive vibes into the world, we can use volition to make it happen. Do not take this as an excuse to lock away negative energy, creating your own ticking time bomb within you. Take this time to use your new breathing technique of six deep breaths. This will help you postpone the real solution of letting the energy out into something else that isn't a person. This is where therapeutic methods of exercise, art, music, journaling, and anything else you can use to let your stress come in. Letting the negative energy out in a safe place where it has nowhere else to go is like defusing the bomb. Better to defuse it than to experience effects similar to the Mechanist's slime, smoke, and stink bombs.

One other method you could adopt is the five-minute rule. Give yourself an isolated five minutes to let yourself be angry or any other negative emotion you are dealing with. Once the five minutes are done, you are no longer allowed to feel that way. Take some deep breaths and move on. During those five minutes, you are allowed to yell, cry, or do anything to let the emotion show. But do not take this out on anyone. Isolating your reactions will be key to not starting a wildfire of negativity. Do not allow yourself to go and interact with people, make it aware you are blowing off some steam alone. If you are talking to someone during this you may cause several problems. One will be that you could make a rash decision that will come to haunt you. The other is that you will unintentionally create a negative wildfire. Even if you don't yell at them, hearing and watching you be in that state could get their own adrenaline going and manifesting some of your negative energy. This method can be a healthy method to deal with bad outcomes at the moment if done correctly. If you misuse it, it could start other problems in the world.

Take the time needed to sort through negative emotions, never ignore them. Take even more priority to put positive energy into the world. One small dose of positive energy can go a long way. Think of how you felt when people did good for you out of the blue. That feeling can be the start to you fulfilling your dreams.

<u>Bringing It All Together</u>

Once you have mastered the techniques in this element, you will be able to help bring positive energy and desire into the world. The emotions of people are contagious. Think of how someone who is smiling at you and genuinely uplifted has changed your current mood. It's how our emotions change with watching a show. Everything around you will influence your fire bending.

While your main focus may be keeping your own fire blazing, you are able to help keep others going as well. Openly share the content that helps shape you in your new daily life. When you see someone straying from their goal, ask them questions to help them get back on it. Bring good energy into the world for others as well as yourself.

Think of Zuko when he was only trying to chase his own honor. Those around him were bitter, even his crew in book one. Once he left to help the Avatar, he used his energy to help everyone be free of the war. He even then focused on restoring the Fire Nation to a more honorable state. The mood of people around him changed. There was no more strife to hold on to everything negative as he let that part of him go.

Now, it's time for you to restore the Fire Nation in your own way. Go out and create the world you dream of with your energy. Be the reason people smile and become inspired. Continue the chain of positive energy. The energy that you create will return to you even greater, helping you reach your Omashu even faster.

Iroh's Wisdom

"You have light and peace inside of you. If you let it out, you can change the world around you."

Taking the time to use what good you have inside you to bring light into the world can go a long way. Light is able to give life to beings around it, giving them the warmth and nutrients that they need. When you use the light already inside you, it is able to do much more than the sun can do. You will be able to help guide people in their day and see hope that may have been missing. A simple act of holding a door or helping someone carry something from their car can go a long way. If people see you sharing your light, they will consider sharing theirs and creating a never-ending pay it forwards into the world.

The Lightning Element

Lightning can be an element of great destruction. Both Zuko and Aang have nasty scars from being hit with it. Both of them were in critical condition and could have died. Do not take a blow from this lightly. Think of these massive energy-driven bolts as negative energy. These will not help anyone directly. If you are sending this towards someone, it has full intention to ruin them. This is more than simply ignoring someone running to the door behind you, this is full of intentional harm. While you may not be on a conquest for this, building up negative energy within us can cause thoughts of harm towards others. The good thing is that you have the power to choose to not shoot at anything. You could be like Mako and use it when he had a job at the power plant, using it in an outlet that won't hurt people- in the end helping people is the outcome. Activities to let out anger can be equivalent to this or putting the raw emotion behind you wanting to help others to not be harmed like you were.

Iroh taught another tool you can use to direct other people's lightning. His redirecting lightning technique gives you the power to aim it elsewhere from you and people. Iroh took this technique from water benders, an element you will learn is vast in its power of healing. Redirect the energy away from people and then use it to power a way to help them. If someone is trying to attack you because of their own personal feelings, take the attack and find ways to use it. This will be situational. You could use this to power your motivation to do more good work in the world or use the resources to benefit your cause. The sky's the limit on what you can do. Just aim at what will help people rather than hurt people.

<u>How You Know You Are Ready</u>

Like before when you evaluated yourself after learning Earth, you will be scoring yourself to see your mastery of Fire. As before, here is a checklist to measure where you are. Each item should be scored on a 1-10 rating. 1 is the lowest indicating that you have nothing and have only read the section. 10 will be the highest and means you are confident in the work you have done in that section and see no more need to improve it. Add up the scores at the end and look at your overall score. Think of it as a letter grade in school, 90-100 is an A, 80-89 is a B, 70-79 is a C, 60-69 is a D and everything below that is an F. The goal here is to reach for an A. While other scores are considered passing, they don't indicate mastery. You could move on in the average level grades such as B and C, though be aware there is a possibility to lose control of your fire and burn yourself as well as those around you.

____ You have journaled and fully evaluated why you must change.

____ You have integrated the necessary material and content to help stay inspired.
____ You have implemented practices of volition and have a firm grasp of the concept.
____ You have come to terms with and let go of the things that do not serve you in your Avatarhood.
____ You have taken positive action to grow in your work.

____ You have worked through any negative emotionally driven motives and created new positive ones.
____ You are consuming knowledge and connections in all areas of your life.

____ You are practicing and finding good progress in taking in
opposing views and choosing with unbiased motives.
____ You are making efforts to help those around you with your energy and see positive effects.
____ You feel confident in how all these work together.

____ Overall Score

Air

<u>What Airbending Is To Us</u>

Daily tasks to succeed should be as simple and second nature as breathing. This is where you will learn to use flow in your everyday life. To turn your mind and body to do tasks at a whim and to stay there. To feel everything moving in the positive direction that you need. This is more than just mindset. This is not only bringing the mind to believe and focus on your journey but to bring the body with it. Almost like muscle memory except the body can freely change courses as it goes through all of this.

Zaheer gives a small speech to the Earth Queen as he assassinates her in the episode *Long Live the Queen*. He tells her, "To your people, freedom is just as essential as air, and without it there is no life." Take into consideration what it truly means to be successful and fulfilled. It is living life, having the freedom to go about as you please, it is having a flow of balance with little to no resistance. It is a basic idea of what everyone strives for no matter their dreams. You and everyone else want to live life in your own way without a feeling of resistance. To get past this resistance and create the freedom that you strive for, you must prepare your mind and body.

Air bending will also give you the ability to not only help control your inner self but to help adapt to the world around you. As much as you may want to change the world, not everything will change for you to get there. If you are stuck in a 9-5 making an average amount of money, you won't be able to solve homelessness by just building homes to rent out for free let alone be able to pay for the maintenance of the place. You cannot force people to donate and volunteer time for these things. You will have to find new paths and ways to make the biggest impact possible. You may have to work with people you are not particularly fond of for a while. You may have to spend crazy amounts of hours for days working on something. Instead of resisting and dreading it, it is a matter of changing perspective.

To achieve these skills, there is a matter of creating awareness. As seen in the Legend of Korra, an air bender can be aware of motion from behind them based on the air from behind breezing over their bald head. They see the world in a more pure light than many, seeing the balance and harmony that is around them. As the other elements are focused on taking action, this element will focus on observing around you. Being aware and present will help you strive further than ever before. Do not worry, shaving your head bald is not a requirement to achieve any of this, though it may be suggested as an advanced step.

The end result of this element is to develop a new respect for life and all things in it. Around us, there is a whole world in motion. There is our family and friends, all the creatures that live in and around our homes, plants that grow in the soil beneath our feet, and even the air that carries all memories from all walks of life. There is more than just ourselves in this world. To benefit the world, a total understanding of what is going on around us is essential. Without this awareness, we cannot put the positive energy we need into the world where it is most needed. Put as much time and energy into this as you would any action you want to make. A lot of harm can come from an action without a full conscious decision.

Characteristics Of An Air Bender

Air benders are traditionally peaceful monks with a thoughtful philosophy of life. Wisdom of the value of life usually comes from the advice of these benders. While there are only a few air benders in the Last Airbender, we are able to see a rebirth of this culture in the Legend of Korra. Between the lost culture and the new forming one, there are remarkable lessons to learn from these masters.

During your time of studying the Air benders, you will learn from Aang, Yangchen, Monk Gyatso, Tenzin, and his children. Other notable airbenders we will take from are the new generation of airbenders such as Bumi and Kia. With these characters guiding the way, many possibilities to reach your airbending potential will be met as you learn from older methods to the newest methods. If you feel like you are having Tenzin tell you that you will give up all your belongings and leave your life behind, look towards the newer methods to find a modern solution to acquire that desired result.

Air benders live differently from the majority of the world, as they are nomadic monks. Since they were babies, they started a path of minimalism, peace, and patience. They train until they are completely competent in their art, then receive their blue arrow as a symbol of their mastery. To them, the arrow represents more than a title or achievement, it represents their personal philosophies as they relate to air and how it moves. They are very in tune with the attributes of their element as air flows wherever it goes, it has no possessions, it helps bring nutrients to the world, it has no bias to anyone as it respects all life. They are not easily suede in their ways as they carry the lifelong commitment they make during their training.

While it is not expected of you to give away all your belongings and money, air benders do live in such a way to free themselves from materialism and the difficulties that come with it. Zahere even exemplifies this to an extent where he even let go of human relationships to be able to achieve flying. None of this is expected of you and more will be on this later to what you can do to help achieve this enlightenment. Though understand that air benders do not wish to be tethered down their belongings, instead want to travel and roam without care of non-essential belongings.

Patience brings these benders to be able to withstand all trials thrown at them. While they are still human and show an outburst of anger from time to time, they are able to approach situations with control. They do not rush, rather encourage those to take their time. As the wind blows at different speeds, the benders are not concerned with trying to change it. They find the best results come when it is time and no sooner than that.

It is worth noting that the majority of air benders are vegetarians. This is by no means a way to try and convert you over to a life without meat. This is an example of their connection with life and how they chose to respect it. Aang struggled with the idea of taking the life of another person, even though that person had caused many others to die and threatened those of the world. The act of taking a life to them is disrespecting the gift that it is. This is such an offensive thing to do in this culture that Kelsang, from Kyoshi's lifetime, was banished from the Air Temples for murdering people with a typhoon, even though it would have saved innocent people's lives. The idea isn't that they may be causing good in the world by ending a life, it is that they do not believe they have a right to make that decision.

They expand their respect for life by welcoming all into their home, offering food to hungry travelers, and any support they can provide. They practice their understanding and compassion when they see those in distress. There is no judging, but rather acknowledging people's concerns and troubles as a part of life. Actively listening until the end where they will suggest advice when expected. They take everything into extensive consideration with enough room to change directions with their opinions when called to. They are never set in one direction, instead will pivot to a new one at the feeling of resistance.

Going off of their tendency to avoid once they feel conflict, take a look at their movements as they air bend. Everything they do is circular. Their arms move in circles, they approach and dodge in circles, they even form many iconic airbending moves in circular fashion such as the air scooter. They will never plow into something head-on, but rather go around. This can create many advantages for you. Consider finding an easier and more efficient way to do something rather than being stuck on a single way, dodging those who try to bring you down. Being able to go full circle with an idea, such as spending money to create more money. You will learn more about these tactics later, for now, just take into consideration how something that is seen as negative, such as avoiding things, can be used to help you.

Finally, let's briefly look at something you have probably been waiting for, air benders meditate. It is the center of their mastery as they are able to control their mind and direct it where they need it. We see Aang meditate after a frustrating day of learning to earth bend, we see him meditate when he is lost on what to do, and he even meditates to connect with the world around him. It is a building block of the abilities airbenders can accomplish, where we see the same extraordinary results from real-life monks. It is more than sitting with your thoughts for hours, not moving, and potentially making your back hurt. It is a practice to focus, breathe, awareness, calm the self, and center your mind, and much more than can be put in a single paragraph, or maybe even a book. Do not dread the idea of meditating, how to avoid it, or make assumptions now of how you will dislike it. Instead, go about the training as an air bender, and when it comes time to learn about it, open your mind to the possibilities it can bring you.

<u>Recognizing Attachment</u>

While airbending monks do not have belongings to feel attachment like we do, it isn't always practical to just get rid of your belongings and become a nomad. You also may be on this journey so that you may buy the handful of things you've always dreamed of. No one signed up for this journey to become a monk, but there is still much we can learn from this. Really dive into this and prepare to evaluate your relationship with your belongings.

Being overly attached to belongings can cause obsession, greed, and lots of aggression within yourself. Many times we see these sorts of things as the main characteristics of villains. The Earth Queen in the Legend of Korra was very attached to money and her belongings in her palace. It took away all hope of compassion for her citizens. This is not the way of an air bender. Their philosophy is that everything they have can be shared with others. Aang demonstrated this as he let Toph eat his lychee nuts and borrow his staff in the episode *Bitter Work*, saying that he is happy to share anything he has. Even though he felt resistance when Toph used his staff incorrectly, he held onto that philosophy. When Kelsang lost the toy clay turtle to Kyoshi when she was a little girl during the airbending Avatar test in the Kyoshi novels, he let go of the attachment of the toy even though it was important to his culture. He felt that it would be wrong to take something away from someone who has so little. Air benders see belongings as a way to help others rather than to please themselves.

Do not fear that this means you now have to loan your belongings out every time someone asks. Instead, look at the things you own and evaluate why you got it and if the purpose is being met. Are your collectibles taking over your life by trying to get more and more, or are they something that brings true enjoyment that you can display to share the enjoyment with others? Journal about all of this, get to the root of the relationship with your belongings. This includes money.

Journal Questions
- What belongings do I feel attached to?
- Why do I have things I do not feel attached to? Am I attached to a feeling of having these?
- Is the attachment a positive or negative one?
- How is my relationship with money?
- Is my attachment with something hindering my progress in my journey?
- Why do I want the things that I want?
- Is the purpose of my belongings being met?

You could go on and on digging deep into your relationships with your belongings. The goal is to see if you have a healthy attachment to something, making progress in your journey hard. In this case, start to detach from it. Situations could be something along the lines of you feeling that you need something to prove you are better than someone. In that case, the purpose is to hurt someone while focusing on boosting your ego. This will take away compassion from the things in life that really do mean something to you. It is fun to have things, to live in a nice house and have luxuries. The idea is to not have those to benefit your status by showing someone up. Many times, we can hide behind a mask of materialism, thinking that what we own defines our success and worth. It is not true, what will define you at that moment is your need to protect yourself with things. Work on the why when buying and owning things to make owning things not a toxic way to put up a wall to protect yourself. True humility happens outside the walls we put up, in the open where we can be vulnerable with those we connect with.

Going deeper into the attachment to wealth, know that it is not bad to want money or want to be rich. It can be an inspiration that can be used for good and fulfillment under the right circumstances. The first circumstance is to make sure the money does not become an attribute of who you are. With this in mind, think of what happens to rich people when they lose it all. They go into despair and a loss of identity. They no longer see the worth in themselves as they once did. Look at Prince Wu when he lost his royalty treasures when being crowned in the episode *The Coronation*. He wanted the spectacle and luxury of royal life, not the responsibility of it. When the crown was taken from him when Kuivera refused to step down and there was only a broach for his crowning, he lost himself in self-pity over the lost treasure rather than the loss of his kingdom and people. There was no drive to want to get the people back to help and lead them.

The air benders, on the other hand, worked tirelessly to help the kingdom for no money. Not to say not having money is the way all the time. Their choice of separation from pay helped them not be put in a situation where they would be corrupted by greed. They just wanted to help those by bringing food and helping in all the ways they could. So, when you look at your reasons for wealth, what are they? Are they so you may use the money to help others in the future? Maybe you want just enough to make sure your own family has enough to go to college and has emergency money. The idea is to not be so attached that you keep accumulating more and refuse to spend it. In that concept, no one who needs it will get it. Are you buying things with it to get people to be impressed and amazed? Journal through your money relationship. This could separate you from a path of hoarding it, creating yet another wall to hide behind.

Journal Questions
- How do I view money?
- What was money like growing up?
- How did I hear my parents talk about money?
- Why do I want money?
- In what ways could I help the world around me if I have more money?
- What could change in my life if I had more or less money?

Go deep and get to the root of your relationship with money. While it can help you live, it can ruin your life if you become too attached to it. The idea is to get to a relationship with it where you don't lose yourself if something were to happen to it. Instead, you will look at the situation as one you just need to reconquer. Money is merely an object, it is not a characteristic of who you are.

Going forward, let's take a quick look at the attachment to the past. Holding onto painful memories. False perceptions of who we are.

People who have hurt us. This won't be the only time we look at the past in this way. You will learn healing in your waterbending training that will help the wounds these may have placed. For now, become aware. Journal about what memories you are too attached to and are holding you back now. This could be a death, a fight, a tragic incident, something traumatic. Anything that has hurt you and you still hold onto to this day. Think of Aang coming to terms with how he ran away when he was scared of being taken away from his teacher. He abandoned the world and lost his people. He finally told the story in the episode *The Storm* and found himself starting to heal from that. For now, be Aang during that storm when he let out the regret he had been carrying.

It will be the same if you hold onto memories of how something used to be. There is still hurt in that. Though you know deep down it won't go back to how it used to be. Aang was able to bring people into the Air Nomad way of life, though the temples were never the same as there was less wildlife, no one who was there before, and no one else could air bend. He ended the war that killed his people, yet it did not bring them back. It is the way life goes and it is an attachment that can become depressing and frustrating at the same time. Notice the attachment, notice how it affects you now. Wait for your water bending training to begin healing.

Journal Questions
- What memories am I holding onto?
- What will happen if I don't move past them?
- Why am I holding onto them?
- How will I feel if I let them go?

The last attachment you need to look at is relationships. This will not be past relationships, but rather your current relationships. This is not saying you must end relationships with everyone. You do not have to become Zahere when he is able to enter the void and fly. Instead, look for the attachment to those that hurt you. Excuses come out often when you try to justify why you still hang around someone when they keep on hurting you. This could be in any relationship from romantic, friendship, family, or even work. But remember when we tackled the fact that people who do not serve us due to their negative energy must be distanced from us. It's going deeper into that. You cannot grow and be the person you want to be if you allow yourself to be attached to a false perception of this person and continue to drag them along. You deserve better, and you will do better without them. Continue to always evaluate your relationships and who these people really are. People and relationships can change, it is important to know that one won't be tagging along just to bring you down.

Journal Questions
- What active relationships need to be looked at?
- How do I feel when I am around/ speak with each one?
- What are they bringing to the relationship?
- What am I bringing to the relationship?
- Is this relationship serving me?

The Flying Element

You don't have to necessarily go through your girlfriend's imploding to reach this state. This state will come gradually as you let go of what you don't need to succeed. You will feel lighter as you go through the process of letting go. This includes physical objects you are overly attached to, relationships that are toxic, and thoughts that plague you. It is a process to let go of all of these as you have read, though this element will become a feeling you will start to feel after intense training in the air element. This top element technique is created by holding onto nothing, though you are not expected to let go of everything in your life. Instead, feel lighter as you let go of things that do not serve you. It will be as if you are flying at yourself to not attach yourself to the things that create unnecessary stress. Breathe and feel the results of mastering air bending.

<u>Becoming An Observer</u>

Being able to use air bending to its fullest intent, you must be able to take a step back from life. Removing yourself from the action will allow you to not only learn from what's going on around you but also be able to create deeper connections as you truly bring in the information being given to you. This training will have a few different components to it as being an observer means more than just people watching. Here you will learn how to take from what you see around you as well as how to get more out of conversations with people around you.

To start this off, take a few moments to pause reading this and take in everything around you. Take in all the sights you can, looking at details you've never noticed before. Close your eyes and listen to the sounds around you. Concentrate on the smells that are lingering in the air. Feel the surface you are sitting on, feel for all the crevices it holds. Slowly breathe through your mouth, taste the air that travels over your tongue. Spend several minutes exploring your five senses to take in your environment like never before. Become present and aware of life around you.

Once you are done with this opening exercise, take a piece of paper and a pen to write out what you have experienced. Make sure you go into detail on the new information you brought in. Try to not make it about how you felt during it, instead look at it as the world is. Once you have completed that, it is time to start moving forward to make these kinds of observations more frequent in your life.

Air benders are naturally more observant in their air bending style as they move in circular formations. This is not only a dodging tactic as it then gives them a chance to see all around the room while also keeping an eye on their opponent. This knowledge helps them plan ahead on how to use their abilities more effectively. Aang once used his air bending to make a funnel that shot out coal. This cleverness during the fight helped defend against fire nation guards. Air wasn't enough for Aang to aid in this fight, adding the elements that were around him helped him become an asset to the rebellion.

While you won't be going up in a fight against anyone physically, you will be going up against challenges in other ways that observing will benefit you. Take for example that you are trying to make your business more efficient. You may have several employees under you that do various tasks. By observing, you may find that certain people are better at certain tasks. By taking this into account, organizing them to do such tasks may lead to not only a more positive workplace, but then you know for sure things will be done correctly. If you just send everyone to do something in a fashion that just divides the work without the true intent of the person, you may be putting someone who is less qualified or even may rush through a task that will have to be dealt with again later on.

Beyond this, you can use this in any daily situation as you observe best times and people for optimal efficiency. Observe busy times in the day in the world, people's schedules, and different routes to reach places quicker. Opportunities can come out of anything if you slow down to see. Tenzin learned this as he was getting caught up with Republic City politics, training the Avatar, and reconstructing the Air Nation. When he stopped to watch Korra perform in the pro-bending arena, he was able to see that it wasn't a distraction for her, but an excellent teaching tool for her to be able to put new techniques to work. Many times, it is hard to see past our own methods that we fail to see something new that may reach someone and the goal even fast.

Begin your training by taking a new way to work, a friend's or anywhere you go often. Oftentimes people get stuck in a routine, they begin to be on autopilot where they don't pay attention to them anymore. This is the sluggish and stale actions that will cause you to miss the world's activities. While taking a new route, take in everything you see and hear. You may find a new restaurant you want to try or a park to go to at some point. Beyond those discoveries, you will be opening up your mind to be more active. The mind will be warmed up to look around itself and take in as much as it can.

Go beyond this by going somewhere completely new, even bring a friend to deepen the experience. The big idea is to get out of a box where you only see the same things. For a world that is as big as it is, it's impossible to grow from the small places people routinely keep themselves in. When possible, travel to new places and experience their culture and sights. The more you see and take in the more open your mind will get. Suddenly, your one-track focus on doing things your way will expand to a plethora of ideas.

Now, back it up to be a bit more interpersonal. Our connections with people can be some of the greatest blessings we have in life. The question is, can it grow deeper? It can. There can be more than just knowing basic interests and facts about a person. Typically when asking how someone is, the answer is a pre-scripted answer that you could get from anyone. You may get a little bit of a longer answer, though is it really creating a deeper connection with the person? There are chances that it is not. It's just more information and you move on. Being an observer can help you deepen it though.

This is usually not referred to as observing, but active listening. This version of listening is the act of completely listening to not only what they are saying, but to understand the complete message they are trying to convey. Many times we may hear people talk about something stressful and we blow it off as "that's rough buddy." Not much more thought is put into it, or maybe too much thought is put into it. With active listening, the person will feel truly heard and feel not only appreciated but that you are someone they can talk to about anything. If someone feels that they need to close you off, chances are the connection isn't where they need it to be to trust you with their more personal struggles and endeavors.

Think of Aang as he is listening to Katara and Zuko planning to go and find the man who killed Katara's mom. In the episode *The Southern Raiders*, Aang had already heard much about how she had lost her mother before this point. At the moment she tells Aang why they need to borrow Appa, Aang does not lash out based on his own beliefs. He asks questions to get a deeper understanding and related his own experiences. He encouraged her to go on the trip saying that this is a journey she needs to feel closure. He did try to explain why revenge wasn't the answer, but he never lashed out but let her choose for herself what to do. In the end, she spared the man's life.

Communication is a crucial part of people's daily lives. It influences how we go about things. When people order you to do something you start to feel resistance. Think of when your parents would make you clean your room, it wasn't a pleasant experience. Think of how the experience was when you chose to clean your room. There was a feeling of control and freedom. The same will be done here to connect with people so that you may benefit from the relationship instead of letting it struggle.

Begin the active listening process by intently listening to everything they say. Do not be on your phone or watching something, look at them with full concentration. Remove the phone from the room if it is possible. Looking at someone as they speak is the first indication to them that someone is actually listening to them. From there, stay quiet and listen until they are fully done talking. A trick to this is to wait a few seconds afterward to make sure they said everything they wanted to say. Then, if you don't fully understand something, ask questions. Do not interrupt to ask questions, this will fluster them as they may be getting to that piece of information. Think of a time you were explaining something to someone and they interrupted you, you probably didn't feel great about it and probably lost your concentration on what you were talking about. It can be frustrating to be taken out of the flow as you are passionately talking about something.

If you ask a question in the middle of them talking, it is an indicator that you are not actually listening, you are thinking of what you are going to say. When you are thinking about what you are going to say, it is impossible to bring in everything they may say, as well as you will not truly get the feeling of why they are doing something.

Having people repeat themselves takes a lot of energy out of them, especially if it's an emotional topic. So, in response, they are a little more hostile, then giving you negative energy where you two can build on that and end up having negative feelings about each other for a time. These interactions build up over time and may affect how you see them as well as how they see you, endangering the relationship.

If you find that you are having difficulty paying attention as someone speaks, maybe your mind wanders or you start to think of what you want to say by accident, try repeating what they say in your head as they say it. This will bring your focus onto their words. Active Listening will take practice if you are not used to doing this. But doing so will give you enough information to make better calls when communicating to people.

Once you have heard and understood what the person is communicating, do not tell them what they should do. Instead, you may ask more questions to learn more, though make it clear they do not have to talk anymore about it if they do not want to. If you feel like offering up advice, ask if you may suggest something. If they consent, then proceed. If they decline, drop it. Telling someone what to do will not let them feel heard, rather they will feel forced into having to do something a certain way even if they don't feel comfortable doing so. Think back to the cleaning bedroom scenario earlier discussed.

Once the person feels it is time to stop talking about it, drop it. They have reached their limit for the time being and needed to recharge. You must likely give them a space they never get to be in, one where they are heard and not judged. Being quiet, listening, and only inquiring more information to show understanding will deepen the experience. Relating to them will help show your level of understanding, but never make it about you unless the topic is about you. This first step to your training will help give you and others the freedom everyone seeks in their life, to be heard and to make their own decisions.

Uncle Iroh's Wisdom

"Life happens wherever you are, whether you make it or not."

Keep in mind that life is always happening. Even when you sit and do nothing, everything still lives on. You can take yourself completely out of a picture and there will still be life in motion. Life will not stop if you are not there. This is why you must learn to observe and not always be. Life has no pause button and will never rely on you like you think it will. Understanding how things live around you, without you, will give you a perspective you can't get anywhere else. This knowledge will help you truly see what needs to be done and how you need to be the one to step up and solve the problems. If you don't, then there is no guarantee someone will, and everyone's life will go on with the problem.

<u>Meditation 101</u>

    This section may be new to you. Meditation is often shown in a comedy act of boredom, weird ohms, and a practice only spiritual beings will do. These are misconstructions to the true beauty of meditation. Here we will talk about a few forms and benefits of meditation. If you enjoy and find great pleasure in the meditation described here, look to the resource section for more information.

    Meditation is a very old art with no certain origin. There has been literature from 1500 BCE India referring to Dhyāna or Jhāna as the practice of training the mind. This practice is translated to meditation most of the time. Meditation practice has also been traced back to the 3rd century BC in China. Nothing points to the true origin

106

point of this practice. There have been significant contributors in the art that have helped spread the practice such as The Buddha, Loa Tzu, and Dosho.

No religion owns meditation. It can be traced to Eastern religions, and oftentimes that is what comes to mind when you think of it. Truth is, there had been traces of it found within religions of Christianity, Judaism, and Islam. Each culture puts its own spin on the practice. The main focus of meditation isn't a religious one, though it can help in your religion and spiritual life.

Before we start the action of meditation, consider why the Air Nomads meditate. Meditation calms the mind and helps control our thoughts. When thoughts race in our minds there is a feeling of anxiety, anger, and depression. Many times turning us away from the actions we need to take. Meditating is essentially training for the mind. In that quiet time when you are left with your mind, you are not exactly facing your thoughts. You are acknowledging that they are there and going back to a focal point to focus your energy on. This will clear the mind as you are not letting thoughts run rampant.

There are techniques in meditation to help you achieve a calm and controlled mind. There are breathing techniques to control the reactions of your body. The breath is the root of emotions. When you are anxious, you breathe faster and shallow. By slowing your breath, you will naturally make anxiety decrease, giving your body the opportunity it needs to calm itself. Think of the six deep breath exercises from the fire element. The deeper, slower breaths cause the heart to slow down as well as the entire body. Your focus on breathing brings your focus away and to a new mindset.

To begin meditating, find a quiet spot where you can sit in an upright posture. You may lay down while meditating, though you could risk falling asleep. This can be in a chair or the ground. Find a comfortable position where your back is up straight, do not slouch. If you are on the floor you can either cross your legs, butterfly style or even sit back on your legs with your butt resting on your ankles. In a chair, you may just let your legs hang down and feet lay flat on the floor. Once you are seated correctly, move your arms in front of you, palms upward, resting in your lap, and while your hands are upside down, press each finger into its corresponding one. If you are sitting in a chair you also have the option of letting them rest at your sides or on the armrests if that feels comfortable. From there you will close your eyes and be ready to start the meditation.

The idea here is to focus on your breath. Breathe in slowly through your nose for six counts. Then hold for four counts. Finally, release the breath from your mouth slowly for six counts. Repeat this throughout the meditation. The idea is to focus on your breathing, to force your mind to control it and clear itself out. If you get a thought other than this, do not get flustered or panicked. Like a balloon full of air, a light tap will send it away in a new direction. Acknowledge that it's a thought, then gently push it away as you return to your concentration on your breathing. It may take some time to get the hang of it and to be able to fully move on from the thought. Do not get discouraged from this and continue to practice meditating.

At first, you won't be able to or expected to go as long as we see the airbenders meditate for. It can be excruciating at first to go for long periods of time. Start with a goal of five minutes. After a while try to tack on another five minutes and so on. There is no right amount of time to meditate, it is a matter of preference and experience. The longer you can go, though, the bigger the grasp on control of your mind. This kind of mastery can take years. Do not expect yourself to be at that level in a month or so. The idea, for now, is to start control through meditation.

There are other ways to meditate than what is described above. Two other ways that will be talked about here are guided meditation and mala beads. These two meditations have in a sense the same goal as a standard meditation, though have their own benefits. In the end, it's up to you to find what will work for you. You by no means have to do all the ways, though at least one way is recommended.

Guided meditation in a sense could be seen as when the Avatar meditates in a highly spiritual place with a guide to then be able to communicate with spirits, or even enter the spirit world. Well, the idea is the same. Guided meditations are meditations that will literally guide you through a meditation. They will talk you through it, telling you exactly what to think, see in your mind, feel, and smell all of it. Usually, when you select a guided meditation, it can have a specific subject such as targeting anxiety or getting energy.

Finding guided meditations is relatively easy. You could find someone who gives classes or sessions in person. Or you could look online. The internet is full of different kinds of guided meditations that range from 5-10 minutes. Sometimes even longer if that is what you are looking for. The key to these is finding one with a calming voice that will work for you. If you want a guided meditation for positive thinking, put it into the search bar with the terms guided meditation. You will have hundreds of videos to choose from. Typically they will tell you how to position your body. It can be nice to focus on someone's words to guide you through the practice.

Even if you like to do guided meditation, a recommendation is to also find time to also practice the basic meditation described before. This technique relies on an outside source guiding you through. If in any case, you need a meditation session when you are out in about because you are getting anxious, you would have to listen to one in some way or form. If you are also practicing meditation that you can do on your own, then in these situations you can just step aside and do it yourself.

Mala beads in meditation are a different type of guide. This is a physical object you will need to obtain. It is a necklace with beads referred to as mala. The closest thing we have to this is the necklace Aang wears after the war ends. His necklace also has beads and pendants of the elements on it. His is designed to have the element pendants act more like the beads will for you. When Aang is holding a certain element while meditating, he is able to contact a past Avatar with the corresponding element. He does this in the Avatar comic, *The Promise* as he contacts Avatar Roku for advice. For you, the mala bead necklace has 108 beads and can be found online for a relatively cheap price. Selecting a type of mala bead does not have to be a big ordeal, though the meaning behind different materials used is interesting. In the end, the important part is having 108 beads.

To use them, sit as described before with basic meditation. Instead of putting your hands together, grasp the bead next to the tassel. This will be your starting bead. Then close your eyes and focus on your breathing for about three to five minutes. Once you are focused, pay attention to the beads, holding only one at a time to repeat a positive affirmation out loud. For instance, you could do "I am happy." for the first one. Then move to the second and say that phrase again. Do this for each bead until you get back to the tassel. Once you get to the end, you have three options: focus on your breath for a longer meditation, choose another affirmation and go around again or end your meditation.

The objective of this meditation is to say something enough times that it essentially brainwashes your mind to think that. It may take multiple sessions, though compare your mood on the days you do this to the days you do not do this. With that in mind, this works best if you do it just after waking up. Your brain will still be in a state called the Alpha state, where you are connected to your subconscious. This can also seem to happen when you are in a daydream-like state on a commute, where you seem to blackout and can't remember what just happened over the past few minutes. This is the stage where you can feed your subconscious so that it will work for you in the long run.

The downside to this, and a reason it will be also recommended to do basic meditation as well, is that it is a meditation that works best at a certain time of day with a specific object. It can be done outside this time zone, though it won't be as effective. You could carry the beads in your bag, though remember this method requires you to speak out loud. Having the basic meditation practice ready for situations out in daily life can be useful as you don't need anything but yourself to help get through moments where you need to control your mind from negative thoughts and energy.

Uncle Iroh's Wisdom (But kind of from Zuko this time)
"You must look within yourself to save yourself from your other self. Only then will your true self reveal itself."

As confusing as Zuko made Iroh sound, there is still truth to unpack here. You will never know your true self unless you look inward. Meditation can be a great way to do so as well as journaling. Once you look inwards, you can control yourself from the person you think you are. The person you think you are may be a complete lie. How many times have you thought of yourself as dumb? It's not true, you are not dumb. But your inner self needs to overcome this being that believes it. Once the fake self is destroyed, you can truly show who you truly are to the world.

<u>Positive Affirmations</u>

The mala beads were just an introduction to positive affirmations. As you focus on strengthening your mind, it will be important that it is getting the right programming. Here we will go deep into the ways that our words are the true programming of our minds and how you can use that to your advantage. It is no secret that the Air Nomads are strong in their beliefs that bring them to enlightenment, now it's time for you to do the same.

The reason the words we say are so important is the weight they carry on us. If you say something enough times you will be brainwashing your mind to think that way. Think of it as faking it until you make it. While the affirmation you say may not be true yet, you can speak it into existence. This can be for physical objects, accomplishments, or your mental well-being. During this section, think about what needs improvement in your journey. This could be mental illness, financial situation, body image, and much more.

Journal Questions
- What do I need to improve in my life?
- How do I currently talk to myself when faced with these situations?
- Would I talk to a friend like that and why?
- Where do I see myself heading if I keep talking to myself like this?
- How will I change the way I think and talk to myself?

After completing these, you will be ready to proceed with the work needed to change how you think. Being aware is only the first step. Now you must accept that it needs to change. If you don't believe it needs to change, it won't. You will have already sabotaged any chance of change. What you think will become reality.

Once you are ready and fully accept the fact you must change in the areas you discovered, you are ready to start the journey to changing those thoughts to be positive and enlightening. Your first task will be one that happens when it happens. Pay attention to when you say harmful things to yourself. For instance, if you call yourself stupid. Take a moment to notice what you said and say "I am smart" three times. Even if at that moment you do not believe it. If you say it enough, it will pop into your head more often down the road and you will see that you actually are smart.

Once you start to get into the groove of catching your negative self-talk, take it to the next level. Catch yourself when you talk about anything else in a negative context. For instance, "I have to do dishes" will then become "I get to do dishes." This will start to change the appeal and drive to do certain tasks. When we don't want to do something, we feel resistance and want to drift away naturally. This is how tasks like sending an email can be delayed three months. Instead, program the mind to think that doing these tasks is a privilege. Not everyone gets the opportunity to do dishes because of circumstances, but you do. Remind yourself that as you go through life and use that to help the mind, choose to do the things you don't want to do. If you mess up and accidentally say you have to do something, don't get frustrated, just do like before and say "you get to" three times out loud. Eventually, your word choices will naturally change and give a new context to your mind.

Now, take this to the next level. Write down affirmations that you most need to program into yourself. If you are struggling with believing you're intelligent then write down "I am smart" on a sticky note or any piece of paper that you can hang somewhere you will see it daily, multiple times if you can. This could be on your bathroom mirror, bed stand, car dashboard, your desk, or anywhere. As long as it's in the open where you have to look at it. Put it in multiple places as well, the more you see it the quicker your mind will be influenced by it. You could even write it on your mirror with an erasable marker. Take it to the ultimate level and put it as your lock screen on your phone or computer. Always be vigilant to find the perfect places for your affirmations to be posted.

If your affirmation has to do with a specific location, put it there. If you are trying to lose weight and trying to stop calling yourself fat, put the affirmation in the kitchen. This will remind you what you are striving for when you go to select something to eat. It may even ward you off when you are about to eat because you are bored. Location can be key to associating your goals with the mindset that you need.

There will be some affirmations that may seem weird to do, and you should look to find the alternative that will fit your narrative better. For example, let's say you struggle with depression. You want to use positive affirmation to help fight it, but saying that you aren't depressed feels like you are lying about something serious that you need to also have other help for, almost like you are denying that it's there. Do not start saying that you are not depressed and stop seeking other forms of help. Instead, say something like "I am getting help for my depression." You don't have to deny ever having it or that it's something you are struggling with, find the statements that will be progressive for you. Try others such as "I'm getting better everyday" "I had depression and now I make sure to take care of myself to not go back to that mental state" and "I'm fighting depression off." This overtime will keep your mind in the zone to continue to work at overcoming it. Though these are not replacements for therapy and other medical help to get past it, it is a way to help bring your mind to where you need it.

Affirmation Card Exercise

Affirmations should be something you can carry with you at all times. This exercise will involve you making a small paper card with an affirmation that you can carry in your wallet or purse to be able to read whenever. On the card fill out the following statement "I am a _____ who is _______, _______ and ________." The blanks can be anything you want to remind yourself throughout the day.

Uncle Iroh's Wisdom

"In the darkest of times, hope is something you give yourself. That is the meaning of inner strength."

Inner strength is when you push forward even when people say to give up. If you hold onto hope within yourself you will be able to keep going. Think of those that have striven through hard times. They had to give themselves hope to make it to the other side of the dark times. You can do this by feeding the hope within you and using your willpower.

<u>Be The Leaf! - Adapting To Obstacles</u>

Adapting when resistance happens is the natural order of air. If the wind is blowing and it comes across a tree, it will simply blow around it instead of through it. Think of Korra's first air bending exercise where she must go through a field of spinning platforms without hitting them. Tenzin explains the concept to be like the leaf and follow the flow of air, when you meet resistance simply change directions. When going through adaptation, think of the line Meelo yells to Korra as she attempts it, "Be the leaf!"

As you go about being a leaf, once you feel resistance in life, go in a new direction to reach where you are striving. There will be two types of adaptation during this training. Obstacles and circumstances. Think of them as obstacles being temporary and circumstances being everlasting. For now, we will focus on obstacles. You can imagine Tenzin's obstacle course for the new air bender's training in *The Legend of Korra*. You cannot keep going straight through an obstacle, instead, you must do something different to get past it.

In your life, you may come across having to work a full-time job while working on your dream job at the same time to make the dream job one day a full-time job. That would be an obstacle. You still need money to support yourself and your family. If the full-time job disappeared, you would lose that as you are not ready to be full time, for example, a musician. As you practice and look for people and gigs to work you will keep up the job you no longer want. It does take up time and energy, though by using free time to work on your music you will be able to one day quit the full-time job you hate to be a full-time musician, then clear up that time again and not be miserable.

It can be the same kind of concept as money. If you need money to purchase equipment for your dream job, but you simply don't have some to spare, you could adapt to cutting out things like streaming services and other things you don't need to spend money on, work overtime, or get a second part time job where you put that money aside for the equipment. The resistance is not having money to buy the equipment, the new direction is the way you will get the money to do so.

When evaluating resistance, ask yourself where you are stuck. If you are building a deck from scratch, it may seem that you can do it all yourself. If you've never built one before, you may find the stringers for the stairs are a bit tricky from scratch. One wrong thing and they are useless. Instead of getting it done in a few days, it's been a few weeks and you don't seem to be making progress on it. You mess up and sike yourself out. You only have so much money to buy wood to make them. Start evaluating where the resistance really is. In this case, it could be the fact you want them from scratch. Maybe you are too proud to ask someone for help. You keep going forward the same way that is taking longer than it should have and you still don't have steps for your new deck. Be the leaf and drift to a side to resolve this issue. It could be buying a pre-cut stringer from the lumber store or asking a friend who has done this before.

It won't always be easy to want to be the leaf. At times pride can make someone want to do it their way or hit the highway. But if you do that, then you may never get to where you are going. Think of Tenzin when he had to guide Korra into the spirit world to close the spirit portal. Tenzin had never been able to meditate into the Spirit World before, yet the situation came up where it was now or put the world in jeopardy to Unalaq. They tried many different methods, yet he couldn't do it. He was resistant when they suggested that Jinora guide Korra. Tenzin hit resistance by not being able to send Korra to the spirit world and a solution came about, though it would cause Tenzin to feel resistance towards his pride and fatherly nature to protect his daughter. He did let her guide Korra, where they easily meditated into the Spirit World with no resistance.

Learn from Tenzin. If they had more time and less urgency, maybe he could have eventually been able to guide Korra. But he knew if he didn't let Jinora, guiding Korra to the Spirit World wouldn't happen. He had to fight his inner resistance to get by the physical resistance in front of him. Take time to find the root of the resistance and guide yourself to the smoothest path. Journal about it. Ask yourself if there is a part of you resisting the change you need. It could be pride, spite, or any other negative emotion that likes to sneak up on people. Those are only obstacles. You can get through the course just like the air benders eventually did.

Journal Questions
- What resistance are you facing?
- Is it temporary or permanent? (If permanent leave those off to the side until you have read and started journaling about circumstances.)
- What are ways I could accomplish this obstacle? (List them)
- What are the pros and cons of each solution?
- How do I feel about the most effective way? (This is where you really evaluate any resistance you have about the best way.)

Be The Leaf!-Adapting To Circumstances

Being the leaf in circumstances can be harder to do than an obstacle. An obstacle you can see the end while a circumstance won't have one necessarily. This is where you will feel resistance from something that won't change. For instance, having children could be one. There is resistance towards going for your dreams because you don't want to be selfish and give less time to your kids or you don't want to risk being a parent that cares more about their jobs more than their children. Being faced with this resistance though can be turned into the opposite if you "be the leaf".

Start with the resistance of thinking that this circumstance will take away from them. Tackle and journal about how you going after your dream will help bring them a better life and inspire them to live a life they are happy in, instead of doing something that makes them unhappy. Break down why you have the resistance and how you can flip that. Having this mindset will open multiple different opportunities for you. With this, you will allow the paths for your leaf to take to open up and be visible to you. This may have been a topic you tackled earlier in a different element, but take time to look at it again. The clearer you are about it the better results you can achieve.

Journal Questions
- What circumstances am I facing?
- What do I currently think of them?
- How can I flip this way of thinking?
- Will my life be better if I overcome this circumstance?

From there, look for opportunities to adapt to your secret tunnel and Omashu. When looking for time, find when you could get up earlier or stay up later. The time when your partner or someone could take the kids for an hour or so. Prep all meals to open up time throughout the week. It will feel like you are still resisting something due to the amount of work that is still required, though compare it to the resistance you would have felt otherwise. The resistance to not go for your dreams, to not have that fulfillment and happiness. That can be a resistance that hurts you in many different ways and won't go away. When adapting to a circumstance, the hard work put into it will eventually bring you to a place where you can drop the parts that are no longer needed and open up more time to do other things you wish to do. You will be playing with balance and imbalance again like before. To become imbalanced is an opportunity to strengthen your balanced life.

This can be used in more circumstances than having kids. It could be a disability you have or a relationship that has been permanently changed. There will always be events in your life that you cannot change or reverse the effects it has on your life. If you face a separated marriage with shared custody, there isn't much you can do about that majority of the time. It's a matter of adapting to it in a way to protect your life in the direction you want.

Aang could not change the fact that his entire people were murdered. He could have given up in despair, refused to step up as the Avatar. There are many ways he could have let that guide him. He stepped up and created a world where he could start the first ripple to save his culture. He had Tenzin and taught him everything. There were no finding others, it was a matter of working with what he had. Air acolytes in the temples helped carry the culture and history. While they could not air bend, there were sides of the culture that could then still live on. He not only had that as part of his Avatar legacy but also was able to work off of that to be the Avatar. Acolytes could teach new acolytes the culture. He created a ripple effect and did what he could on the side of his Avatar duty.

To sum up, this section, find ways to incorporate your Omashu and purpose into your current circumstances. Do not try to change what cannot be changed and do not give up due to the fact. Instead, find the path that works around it. Be the leaf and change directions once you feel resistance in your journey. It is not worth the energy to fight against what won't budge.

<u>Your Relationship With Life</u>

This is where you understand the purpose of the air bender's philosophy and build your own when it comes to the life around you. In a nutshell, you will evaluate how you respect it and how you will continue to respect it. The air bender holds a respect for life at the top of their morals, or you could say they are ground rules if you go back to your earth bending training. They are attuned to the world around them and see life as a gift that they have no power over.

Air benders practice their respect for life in a number of ways. The most prominent one we see them practice is their choice to be vegetarian. Even to the smallest creature, they do not feel they have the right to take a life. If they do, they show disrespect for the gift of life. All life to them is sacred and so should not be tampered with. Even when taking away a life could save the world, they still see that life as a sacred entity that they don't deserve to sever from the world. We watched this as Aang struggled with having to kill the Fire Lord, having to find a new way to take care of him without committing a crime scene by his culture and himself.

Now when looking at your perspective of life around you, what is your own philosophy? Do you feel you respect it enough in your actions? Do you feel you need to make changes in how you look at it and go about it? These are questions you should explore in journaling. Really get deep with it and create strong statements of how you feel and what you want to do to help back that up. You could make giving back to people a higher priority, recycle, feed birds, or whatever you feel is needed. The small actions will grow bigger as you continue to live by what you believe and take action on those beliefs.

Journal Questions
- How do you currently see life around you? Do you need to evaluate it more?
- Where do you see this belief in your own actions?
- What can you do to honor life around you?
- Are you happy with how you treat life around you?

These actions will grow your airbending mastery as you open the world to yourself. If you go about your life with the one-track mind of yourself, not caring about everything around you, you can do much harm. If the air only traveled one way in a certain strip of area, then everything around it would wither. There would be nothing to carry oxygen to it, to bring carbon dioxide to it, to carry seeds to bring more growth, no pollen to travel, and so on. Everything outside of that will suffer. A room will grow stale if there is no air to travel through it.

When you give to the life around you, it will return the favor at some point. Together you both can grow to help the world tenfold. One person can only do so much, but with more anything can happen. Aang alone could not end the war, it took his friends and others to finally end it. Even if he took down Ozia, Azula was still at the Fire Nation. Without Zuko and Katara to take her out, there would have just been more. Aang would have had to do to finally save the world.

Do not forget, the job of the Avatar is to bring peace and balance to all. This means all nations, all benders, all non-benders, all spirits, and all living things. If you strive to be a full-fledged Avatar with the intent of not helping those around you, your duty of being the

Avatar is not being fulfilled. Know your own philosophy of respecting life, continue with compassion and an open heart, and always take with you the importance of the gift of life.

Uncle Iroh's Wisdom

"Ick! This is nothing more than hot leaf juice!"

While a funny line, it holds much more meaning to him than what the surface shows. To Iroh, tea is a gift you can have and give others to show love and peace. When he is given a cup, he expects the time and effort to be put into it. He is disappointed to find the warm love and caring that he found in tea is gone. When you do something, bring love into it. Help bring comforting emotions to people. When it is rushed and forgotten, it feels cold and undesirable to people. In the end a waste of both people's time.

<u>Testing Your Patience</u>

Things take time. It's easy to want to snap your fingers and everything to be done and to be at your Omashu. In reality, that will never happen. You must be patient. It takes years for the Avatar to fully master the four elements, the Avatar State and diplomacy. Everything that goes into making this individual takes time. While we see Aang having fantastic skill at water bending, we still see Katara giving him exercises to do when he isn't training on the other elements. We see the time that is put in for air benders to get their arrows when we watch Jinora strive for them. While she was the youngest to receive her arrows, it still took her years to prove her mastery of it. At age ten she was able to get them, but also note how she started as a very young child. It could have been easily 5-7 years of formal training to get to where she could get her tattoos.

You are no different. You have made great strides in your own training to get where you are, but nothing happened overnight. In reality, society is driven by the instant nature of screens and two-day delivery. Everything must happen immediately. There is no having to read for an answer from multiple books, it can be searched in a matter of seconds. Even bypass the typing and ask devices vocally to an instant answer like you were talking to a person right next to you. If you have a message for someone far away, you could just call or even send a text. There is no practice in daily life anymore for patience. Now is the time to start so you don't try and jump the gun when your Omashu doesn't happen right when you finish this book.

Meditation can be one way to help with this. The long silent moments locked in your own space can be hard to do. It takes years to get to a place where people can meditate for hours or even an hour. Take that challenge in your meditation to work on your patience. Learn to handle the frustration when you end it early by accident or when you break concentration. This can be an easy daily way to fit in with patience training. You are already working on strengthening your mind, why not also put more effort into it to test your patience.

Go beyond this and implement the six deep breath method talked about back in the fire element. Every time you feel impatience creeping up on you, immediately start doing that. Get into that habit. Be conscious of what is happening and take action. Being impatient can be aggressive in your emotions. It makes you do hasty things and think negatively. Gently push it away. Remind yourself that everyone is human. All things will happen in their own time. When Korra was frustrated by her air bending training, she let the impatience with her progress get to her and she only acted rash instead of taking the moments needed to do it step by step. In the episode, *A Leaf in the Wind*, it led her to lash out at Tenzin. Once she breathed on the pro-bending arena and calmed herself, she was finally able to do the spiral movements of an air bender and dodge the incoming attacks on her. The moments to stop and breathe and regain focus can be the difference of impatience causing you to fail and patiently do something correctly.

Another way to practice this is to put yourself in situations that will test it naturally. Try baking bread from scratch. You need to allow the yeast to rise as well as all the physical work that goes into kneading the ingredients together. It is not like buying a mix from a box or an already made loaf that is pre-sliced from the grocery store. This will take time. If you are not used to this kind of experience, try it. See what goes into it and practice your patience during it. If you mess up and have to start over, breathe and do it again. Work at it until you have a decent loaf of edible bread. Then enjoy a warm fresh piece of it to show yourself what can happen when you go through without rushing and keeping your cool. If you want an even harder challenge- churn your own butter for the bread!

There are many ways you can continue to practice your patience. Find more tasks like baking bread. It could be building a table from wood, sewing a dress, or even gardening. There are many daily items you use that have to be made somewhere, why not experience that process and then enjoy the fruits of your labor to connect your brain to the satisfaction of the journey when it's done calmly and right.

A method you could try once you are more practiced in the way of patience is to debate with someone. Not argue or fight, to debate. It's easy to be impatient with a person when they are saying the exact opposite of what you believe. When they don't truly hear you. In today's world, you can hide behind a screen and really rail someone for hours. You can start writing your response before they even reply. It's so easy now to lose your cool by just seeing a post you don't agree with. If you feel ready, and your blood pressure is not at stake, find someone to have a friendly debate with.

When doing this, make sure it's in person. Be able to look and listen to them, remember to actively listen. Reading is not the same as listening to someone say something. Text can easily be misinterpreted. Make eye contact and read body language. The goal here is not to win. It is to stay calm no matter what. The rule of thumb is if you are the first one to raise your voice, you lose. Also, if you raise your voice at all during this you will have failed the exercise. Breathe evenly and remind yourself that you cannot change a person's mind, they must decide to do that themselves. If you leave the debate without losing your cool and understanding a little more why someone thinks the way they do, you passed. If you stay calm but ignore most of what they say to avoid losing your cool, you merely lost patience with them the second you stop listening.

In the end, debating can be useful to practice handling much life will throw at you. Being a master debater isn't about winning necessarily, it's about staying calm and listening to the other side. Patience is key to understanding everything around you. Do not do this unless you are for sure ready to handle this type of stress, there is no pause button when talking to people. You must be ready to use it in an intense situation when needed.

Now that you know how to be the leaf, it's time to do the same, but with people. Not in a way where you just don't like being around people, but to avoid those who will only hurt you. Unfortunately, in the world, there are people who play the villain in our stories. They want the opposite of what we strive for, they want you to fail or they just want what you have. Any reason they have, there is no way to not have these people in your life, and oftentimes people may call them haters. Here you could also see them as the villains seen in the series, such as Fire Lord Ozia, Amon, Zahere, or any being that defies the law of balance held by the Avatar. If you wish to even call them by your favorite villain in the series, by all means, it will just make the experience of them more fun.

You don't have to put everyone with any inconvenience to your journey on a pedestal. There are minor inconveniences such as thugs and such, those will be easier to dodge. Look at them who may just complain that you won't pig out with them at a party because you are trying to lose weight. Those you can just simply shrug, give a nonchalant response if you want, and walk away. Chances are they won't follow you trying to stuff chips and appetizers down your throat. If they do, then see them as a higher threat and be stern and again don't engage with them again. If you have to, drive the conversations somewhere else. They can't try and taunt you if you get them on a different topic.

If you are facing someone who is constantly trying to sabotage you by filling your house with easy to access junk food and only talks down to you about what you are trying to do, maybe consider them as more of a villain at that moment. There is no changing their mind, so don't go towards that resistance. Instead, you can limit where your healthier food is, out of reach of others, and separate yourself from the planned sabotage. If they bring up the topic and try to bring you down, tune them out if you have to, walk away, and tell them that you agree to disagree. You hold power over your life and what you want to deal with. If it is so persistent then find a way to not live with them. Your training has come to a point where you have the tools to find new routes, patience, and a strong mind. Now, you need to use them to send away the negative energy by being upfront with people. If they don't back off then you do not have to take their criticism of your journey.

To make it clear, there is a difference between criticism and constructive criticism. Constructive criticism is the kind where you can grow from, the other kind is unhelpful opinions. Those with constructive criticism can be helpful when they honor you for when you are ready to receive it. Otherwise, you do not have to consider much with following through with any opinion.

If you are working online for the public to be able to comment on your work, you will run into some traditional haters that just want to troll you. These haters' comments can hurt, but with your training, you will be able to handle getting past them. If you become defensive, these comments can be hard to bypass. It's a trap to get you to reply and argue with them, to get you to react. If you cannot handle these types of comments, simply delete them immediately. Going down a rabbit hole with these comments can start to get to you, just like what we talked about with affirmations. Do not engage, delete if you must, and move on.

If there are comments coming from the public, it is ok to distance yourself for a bit to regain composure. We see this many times as Aang meditates to work through anxieties such as a rough day of learning to earth bend. We also see it when Aang takes too much

128

criticism, like the fisherman who mentioned how he disappeared and abandoned everyone in the episode The *Storm*, where it became too much and he had to leave. You won't always be at your best to receive negative comments from people, stepping back to handle it is what is important. That is the distance you can use to avoid those trying to hurt you. Regain yourself and move forward.

To help prepare for these types of interactions where you will be face to face with a hater, continue doing everything you have learned in your air bending training. These are the tools you will use when dodging this kind of opponent. If you can master this higher-level technique then you will be able to handle yourself in many situations. You will even be able to control the debate challenge discussed earlier even better. This will give you the power to end it smoothly when you feel it's about to get out of hand or that the other person is only trying to point criticism at you instead of an honest true debate.

<u>Bringing It All Together</u>

At this point in your air bending training, you should be able to use all these new skills simultaneously together to achieve your goals. Now you are to focus on maintaining as well as growing. The foundation of this will be found in your meditation. If you can control your breath then you will always have an upper hand when utilizing your air bending.

In a way, you can consider yourself a nomad, as you can wander around in life and take everything in, a skill not everyone is able to do. Not only will you be trained to notice the small details of life around you, but now you can bring compassion to all things. Use this element to help the world flourish around you as you connect with others, as you strive for the greatness you are destined for.

If at any point you start to feel like you are losing grasp of one of these techniques, practice at it. Journal it out to find what direction you should go. The idea is to use these together to let the air guide you in the direction that will help you achieve your Omashu. As your secret tunnel continues to change to avoid blocks, ease through. Like your fire bending, don't use the energy you do not have to.

To see your new mastery of the element in action, continue to strive for higher ambitions. If you are striving to help the hungry, go about it with your intention to help lives. When you come across an obstacle, flow around it to a new way of tackling the situation. Listen to the stories you hear along the way, find what people need most in their life. Strive to help people in the best way that you can.

In anything you do this element will surely come up when you deal with people and events. The key is to breathe and remember what you have learned. Think of how Aang, Tenzin, Jinora, and all the new air benders would handle a situation. Where should you put energy and where should you just be a listening ear? Determine how a true air bender would react and resolve a situation. If you mess up, remember that you and all air benders are still human. Even Tenzin and Aang have had their moments of outburst. The important part when this does happen is to go back, calm the mind, and learn how to be better.

Before you move on in your elemental studies, take a moment to journal what you have learned about yourself and the world throughout this element. Where you see more freedom in your life, physical or mental, where you feel you can best serve the world now, where you still need to put more work in. Come back to journal often as you go about your Avatar journey, even when you are done training as a full-fledged Avatar, to see where you are in your mental strength. Remember if your mind is not up to par, you won't be able to handle everything that life has to throw at you. This is why you see many benders besides, airbender meditate and focus on the breath, it's because they also know its importance. The airbenders just know how to take it to the next level.

The Spiritual Projection Element

This element is done in meditation. This is a visualization meditation you can do to bring your mind into the situations and life that you want. A way to show it why it wants it and to continue to strive towards it. First, you will sit like it is talked about before for meditation. Breathe for a while and then imagine yourself living the life you want to live, your Omashu. Go through the entire day in this meditation. Imagine the smells, sounds, touches, tastes as well as visuals. Don't rush through it but imagine what getting up would be like. All the activities of the day and the people in your life. Go all the way until the end of the day when you go to bed. Really be present in it. Once you go through the day, breathe a few times, and end the session. This is almost like the affirmations with the mala beads, but with all the other senses. Do this daily, really get the mind to want to strive for that life and to be excited. What you think about will become a reality.

To make this even more advanced and effective, try playing sounds that you would hear during the day, such as a neighborhood you want to live in. Incorporate smells as well. Anything to bring a more physical side to the experience rather than just thinking about it. This will bring you deeper into your visualization. Think of it as the incense when Korra was trying to meditate to the spirit world. The more senses activated, the more you will bring to your mind's drive to achieve.

<u>How You Will Know You Are Ready</u>

Like before when you evaluated yourself after learning Earth and Fire, you will be scoring yourself to see your mastery of Air. As before, here is a checklist to measure where you are. Each item should be scored on a 1-10 rating. 1 is the lowest indicating that you have nothing and have only read the section. 10 will be the highest and means you are confident in the work you have done in that section and see no more need to improve it. Add up the scores at the end and look at your overall score. Think of it as a letter grade in school, 90-100 is an A, 80-89 is a B, 70-79 is a C, 60-69 is a D and everything below that is an F. The goal here is to reach for an A. While other scores are considered passing, they don't indicate mastery. You could move on in the average level grades such as B and C, but be aware that your flow will only be as good as you dedicate to it.

___ You have done the observing exercises as well as routinely practice active listening.

___You have created a meditation regime and practice it with
                purpose.

___ You have evaluated your attachments to things and have let   go of what is not needed.

___You have created and implemented positive affirmation in all aspects of your life.

___You practice being the leaf in obstacle situations and feel
                confident in your ability to keep doing so.

___You practice being the leaf in circumstances and feel confident in your ability to keep doing so.

___You have a clear vision of your philosophy on all life and
                practice respecting it.

132

___You have acquired a firm grasp of your patience and practice maintaining it.

___You are able to avoid those with negative energy who want to bring you down.

___ You feel confident in how all of these can work together and see them improving your life.

____ Overall Score

Water

<u>What Waterbending Means To Us</u>

Water bending is an element that nurtures the world around it. Water is like the blood of the world as it flows through everything with nutrients that all living things need. Think of the animals and plants that need the water to survive. Humans alone are 70% water. Without water, there would be no human existence. It flows through your body as you drink it. It cleans you as it rushes over you. It aids in cooking your food. It can provide transportation. It even helps bring energy to the world. The fluid nature of this basic human need brings more uses to the world than any other element.

With this in mind, water bending to us is a form of healing. Not only will it be used to help heal those around you, but also yourself. Think of it like this, if the water bender does not heal themselves enough first, how will they be able to heal the others? It will be the same with you. You have a foundation of Earth, the energy of Fire, and the Freedom of Air. Now you must have the healing of Water.

Think of the lives Katara alone has been able to save due to her ability to heal with water bending. She saved Aang and Zuko both after they had been electrocuted by Azula on different occasions. Even Korra was able to help heal Bolin after he hurt his shoulder in a pro-bending match. The most skilled water benders are able to heal as well as use their water bending as a fighting tool.

Water is also a dangerous weapon that can drown your opponents and spear them with ice. The different advantages of water are endless as we see water benders who use it to move the water within vines. Learning how to use it in a multitude of different ways will open a world to you to tackle each challenge in its own unique way. You will see as something may work for you, might not work the same for others. You may have to try something else to get the job done, just as Katara used her own sweat to escape a jail cell in the episode *The Runaway*.

Healing will not always look like healing a physical wound. Instead, it will most likely be healing the mental and emotional wounds that are left within a person. These are the results of traumatic events. It is hard to move on from such things, resulting in loss of fight to accomplish goals and dreams. It will take a process, though it is a step that is needed to be able to serve the world better. It may even seem as if you are creating hope at some points. It's hard to think of the water benders without their drive of hope. There is much behind a waterbender that makes their water bending even more effective than you could imagine.

Here we will visit past elements and techniques being brought into full light. Iroh's redirection of lightning is inspired by studying this element and will be explained in a new light to do more than what the fire benders use it for. Think of it as healing with energy and our thoughts. Though you will find there will also be similarities to air as your training with your mind will put you ahead in your training.

Lastly, as water is a healing element, it is also powerful and can take down even Earth over time. While it brings nutrients to many, it is able to also take away from it. The intentions of water bending will strive for greatness to do good, but can easily turn for the worst. You will learn movement and restraint to control it. You will be able to guide others to safety with a gentle push in the right direction as long as you control your power. Move with this element and you will see the impact you can truly make on others.

Uncle Iroh's Wisdom

"Good times become good memories, but bad times become good lessons."

You will always be able to cherish good memories. Bad times seem to plague people, never truly leaving them. Take those times as not bad but as learning opportunities. You may find there is something to learn about yourself or others. Even if something was totally out of your control, there will be lessons hidden waiting to be found. Look for them and use what they teach you. Turn the bad times into your greatest tools.

Characteristics Of Water Benders

Water benders are much like the element they bend. Their movements are fluid in nature with a strong purpose behind each intention. They can be as gentle as a calm spring and as brave and powerful as a massive wave in the ocean. They surround themselves with their element, giving them possibly the ultimate advantage of all the nations. Choosing to live on polar ice caps, they freeze their water to be solid in structure but are able to become flowing water when needed.

When thinking of water benders, characters such as Katara, Korra, Kuruk, Tonraq, and Pakku may come to mind. Each character brings their own personality to the table as they are all extremely different people. Katara can be kind and sympathetic, ready to bring a speech of hope, while also able to stand her ground when it is most needed. Korra tends to be more rash and rushes to use her bending in combat, making it clear at all times her opinion. Then you have Kuruk, an Avatar who is easygoing like a lazy river, keeping hardships to himself. Water benders are all different like water is. You can have fresh or saltwater, calm or rushing, frozen or liquid, out in the open or within a living being, and even steaming hot or cold. The combinations and possibilities are endless, just as the personalities that can come from a water bender.

Keeping their differences in mind, they are all able to connect with the current of the water and use it as an extension of themselves. We see this as they move back and forth and they push and pull with the water. Their focus flows into the water as they pay attention to the detail of how water moves. They keep their form straight, but also enough to be relaxed as their body moves smoothly.

As you see them move in their element, you can see the passion in their eyes. The true connection they have with the water, the moon spirit that moves within the water, and their entire culture. To them, their people are one just like an entire ocean is one body of water. Traditions are held sacred to them. Protection of their friends, family, and neighbors is important to them. The North and South Pole tribes even see each other as a family as they call each other sister tribes. A bond that they are all connected through the waters of the world.

A characteristic that showed itself through the water benders is the mentality to go against what they don't believe in. We see this in the newer generation rather than the older folks that run the tribes. We first see this in Katara when she went to the North Pole to learn water bending, but they sent her to the healing hut to learn, holding onto their own beliefs. She was furious by the tradition of women only being able to heal, challenging Master Pakku to change his mind. We see this as well in Korra as she challenges anything she doesn't agree with. There is no lack of fight within these benders as they want everything to progress and benefit all around them rather than just themselves.

In the end, these benders will fight to the end to protect all that they love. Their fight has no limitation as they will physically fight and heal someone. The passion within them rages like a storm. To master this element, you will have to put yourself in the shoes of a water bender to understand why their bending is an extension of who they are. The capabilities of their bending are endless as they can bend massive waves and the water in our blood.

Accepting The Path To Heal Trauma

You have probably heard of the phrase "You can lead a horse to water, but you can't make it drink." This phrase rings true in this element. You can bring yourself to all of the people and tools you need to heal, but you won't unless you choose to do so. This is no different than when you chose to go on this journey. The act of accepting you have trauma and need to heal from it will be the first step in overcoming it.

Water benders are no strangers to facing their trauma head-on rather than ignoring it. Think of Katara when she talks about losing her mother to the Fire Nation and her journey of dealing with that. In a different experience, we see Korra do the same as she faces the trauma of almost being murdered by Zahere. Her journey included

Post Traumatic Stress Disorder (PTSD) and feelings of self-doubt as the Avatar.

Like these two water benders, you will have your own story that no one can hundred percent understand what you are going through. All a person can do is imagine how much pain and suffering you have gone through. There are people who can give you tools though, many tools beyond this book to face it. You won't be able to heal, though, if you are not dedicated to it. It is not just putting a band-aid on a paper cut. It may be more intense like breaking a bone again to reset it to heal properly. How you will feel once it has healed will be better than when the injury still ruled your body and mind.

To begin acceptance, take out your journal. In it, you may already have your trauma written down from when it was briefly talked about in the air bending section. You do not have to write it all out, especially if you are not ready to handle the realization of it on a piece of paper. Instead, work through just accepting you need to heal from it. What it is is not important right now. What is important is the decision and why you will heal. Think of it as Korra knowing she needs to heal so she can resume her Avatar duties.

Journal Question
- How is my current trauma affecting my life?
- How is my trauma affecting my relationships?
- How is my trauma affecting how I see myself?
- What is my trauma keeping me from achieving?
- Why do I need to overcome this trauma?

Being clear in your journal why you need to heal from it will be part of you declaring to yourself that you will take this journey and dedicate yourself to healing your mind and soul. This can range from many reasons that may be physical, such as you can't sleep or find yourself binge eating for comfort. The reasons may also be spiritual as you feel disconnected from the world and yourself. Emotionally, you may be suffering from depression and anxiety. Your relationships may even be suffering from your defense mechanism wanting to distance yourself from people. You are the only one who will be able to know how this is affecting you and why you need to change that.

If you don't know all the reasons right now, that is ok. Take the time to get an idea of why. As you go through this journey, you may find other reasons you never noticed before. Korra never felt the lingering poison in her body, only the haunting presence of what had happened. She distanced herself from those who love and care for her, became easily discouraged and frustrated by failure, and even avoided the role of Avatar. The poison wasn't the only thing holding her back, though it was a huge part of slowing down her body. When the first attempt to remove it happened by Toph, Korra was not ready to return to the world as she still fought with doubts about her ability to be the Avatar. Once Tenzin's kids found her to tell her of how Kuivera refuses to step down as the leader of the Earth Kingdom, Korra came to terms that she needed to overcome her trauma to help remove the tyrant from power. This moment is when Korra is finally able to remove the poison with her metal bending.

There is a "want" when trying to heal from trauma, but there is also a dedication to needing it. If the reason is that you have trouble sleeping, dig deeper into how that affects you in other ways. This could be from your concentration on your studies, your patience with those you love, or even the overall health of your body. Explore to find the reasons. There is no wrong answer, if that turns out not to be the only thing going on, then you will come to terms with that one, and go

140

through this process again. The more reason you have to choose to heal the easier the process will be in the long run.

From here, try meditating with mala beads if you can. Say an affirmation of how you will overcome your trauma. Continue to do it daily if you can to remind your mind and body what you will do. Remember that words have great power. If you tell yourself you will never get over something, chances are you will not. Revisit the affirmation section of the air bending element if you need to.

If you do not have mala beads, try writing it over and over again on a piece of paper. How physically writing something down can help your brain retain it better can also be as powerful as mala beads. Do not throw away or burn your affirmation. Instead, keep it near so you may pick it up and read it out loud when you can. These acts of repetition will help you with the healing process just as it helped with your journey up until now. Remember that success is not one big victory, it is a bunch of little ones.

Uncle Iroh's Wisdom

"You must never give into despair. Allow yourself to slip down that road and you surrender to your lowest instincts."

This is where you need to stay strong. To give in to your own despair may cause you to lose all your progress. That is how you lose control of yourself and find things are spiraling out of control from you. Once you slip down that road, you will be vulnerable to make choices that will harm you, maybe even destroy you and those you love. When you are face to face with this, fight to keep going and do not consider the idea of giving up on the emotion. Once you are in there it is extremely hard to get out. You must push through onto a brighter path.

Before we get into the phases of the healing process, there needs to be knowledge of what to expect from this book and how it is not the only thing you need. Take this section as a lesson to open up to those who can help, as well as a disclaimer. The lessons in the next few sections are merely tools to help you guide your way through the phases. Tools a water bender can utilize. This book cannot guide you to the ultimate goal alone. Instead, use it as a way to look at the journey ahead to find those that will guide you in your specific journey.

You cannot expect yourself to do everything. It is a fact of life. There is a dying need in many to do it all themselves, though in reality, it won't work out. You may have tools and a vague idea, but that doesn't mean you know how to do everything when building a house let alone be able to put everything together just yourself. Instead, you find those who are experienced and those who are willing to help you. This is no different when you are facing your traumas. They can't experience it like you did, though they are there to help guide you and show the support you need.

Depending on the trauma, it is highly recommended to seek a professional in the subject you are dealing with. For instance, if you are coming to terms with a death that happened, look for a grieving therapist. People train intensively to be able to help those who are hurting. Going to them will open a clearer path as they help you work through it. They will know the questions to ask and have the tools to help you deal with your pain. You may even find someone who knows a better method of overcoming your trauma than anything else mentioned in the coming sections. To rely on yourself and this book only is to shut out the true solutions to your problems.

Korra was faced with extreme injuries and trauma after the attempted assassination Zahere and the Red Lotus did. While she was already accompanied by a healer, Kya, she was sent to Katara. Katara's skills in healing such trauma were superior to Kya's healing experience. Korra went to the person who knew exactly what to do rather than just any healer they could find. Never settle for someone who doesn't know exactly what they are doing. These trained professionals are those who can truly make a positive difference in your life.

If you are hesitant because of a perception of weakness if you seek professional help, then that is where you need to start when looking for specialized help. Hundreds of people may have even told you that you are not weak but strong to ask for help, though that doesn't release the learned habit that you have of your perception of the concept. You must convince yourself. Take the journal back out and work through why you feel that way. As always, find the root of the cause. It may have been an incident where asking for help backfired on you, maybe you heard someone when you were younger say something about how certain people go to therapeutic help, the source can be found if you stop to think and write about it.

Journal Questions:
- What is my current opinion on getting professional help?
- What did I hear people say about it growing up or seen about it in the media?
- How could professionals help me?
- What will happen if I keep trying to do it on my own?
- Why will going to get professional help change me for the better?
- How am I going to start looking at professional help?

Once you have discovered the source, look for how to change that perception. The answer to that isn't some trick that you need to come up with all on your own. You already have all the tools to work on that. Think back to your training of the past three elements. It is up to you to decide on what tool or tools will help you get yourself into a mindset to get professional help. It may not even be a professional's help, but to ask friends or family to help.

One thing you will most likely need even if you have professional help is the support of your loved ones. It may not be easy to be vulnerable enough to ask for it. Go through the process again with them and work towards acquiring at least one loved one's help. After that, asking more will come more easily to you over time.

Uncle Iroh's Wisdom

"While it is always best to believe in one's self, a little help from others can be a great blessing."

In the end, only you need to believe in yourself to be able to accomplish what you want to accomplish. When others are there to share support do not take it for granted. It is truly a blessing to have more than just yourself standing there as you go through your journey. Hold this close to your heart and use it to its full extent. You will feel the energy they give you to help you on your journey. Not everyone gets this gift in life, cherish it, and extend a thank you their way to show your appreciation.

As part of the water bending training and journey, there will be a few sections dedicated to Judith Herman's phases of trauma recovery. This is merely one way to think of it and go about your journey. If this is not a comfortable and plausible way for you then it is encouraged to research and seek the methods that will help you. These phases break down nicely by looking into the healing powers of water, which is why they are being integrated into this element. By any means, if this is not your style, seek your own style, it is what makes this element so amazing. There is never one way to do something and there is plenty more water bending you can learn to help you on your journey.

Earlier it was mentioned accepting the path to go on this journey. In a sense, this will be an extension of that. If you were not able to feel comfortable enough to journal then, this phase will help with coming to the point where you feel safe enough to proceed with something like that. Here is when you will take as much time as you need to prepare for facing the trauma you faced. It could take a few days to a few years to be ready to get out of this phase. During this time, you will be slowly stabilizing yourself to be able to work on it.

Think of Korra's journey to healing from her paralysis and PTSD in book 4 of *The Legend of Korra*. Her pain can be seen as she sees the Air Nation taking responsibility to help unite the Earth Kingdom. Asami offered to stay by Korra's side in the South Pole, though Korra began her new habit of distancing herself. She expands on this more when she doesn't write anyone back. She only later writes a few letters to Asami. Her sleep is affected as she has recurring nightmares of the poisoning. Korra was found on a balcony just sitting there at night by her mother. At this moment, we see her mother beg her to go and see Katara as it had been three weeks since they got back. Korra agreeing to go and see Katara was the moment she started the acceptance process.

The acceptance process for Korra led more into her first session. Katara told her that it was up to her if she got better or not, Katara was there to just guide her during the process. Korra then accepted that she would have to put much effort into the long journey ahead. This is where you are truly entering the first phase of the trauma recovery process.

The goal of the first phase is to acquire safety and stabilization. We know that she has not reached that when Katara has her attempting her first steps. Before she can take that first step, she gets a flashback and falls to the ground. Katara even comments on how "Your body still thinks it's in danger but it's safe here." The solution is to use your mind to work towards that goal of feeling safe. This is achieved by the environment around Korra in the healing hut. It is calming as well as Katara's soft and caring nature. We see that at first, that isn't enough.

After many attempts of trying to walk, we see Korra lash out in frustration. Katara doesn't scold her for it, instead tells her to let her "anger and frustration flow like water." Creating a safer place to express her feelings. Katara then talks to Korra about how she must feel alone as the Avatar goes through a traumatic experience. The words that made Korra reach a new point of safety are when Katara talked about Aang and his trauma with losing his entire culture. His solution was finding meaning in his suffering. With the comfort of this knowledge Korra didn't feel so alone, Korra was able to visualize and overcome her trauma to walk again. This was only a beginning for her in this phase.

As it was mentioned before, it can take years even to reach a point where you can move on to the next phase. It took Korra about three years. She hit a roadblock in her progress in the South Pole and concluded that being in Republic City with her friends would help. In retrospect, this is a great idea. The love and support you get from people can create the safe and stable environment you need. Korra was driven off from the city, though. Her habit of distance came back as she felt the anxiety of what had happened when she was approaching it. She wasn't ready for that phase of processing the trauma.

Korra traveled the world and eventually was guided to Toph. There Korra let out her fears of the world losing its Avatar. Toph could see that her body did not feel safe and stable as it still had metal poison slowing it down. The only way Korra would be able to bend it out would be to fully accept she needs to heal from all of her trauma to be the Avatar again. She struggled with it. Toph brought her to the banyan tree to show her how she was disconnected from the world and her friends. Once Korra saw the air bender children, she was brought with a sense of safety as she was being reunited with friends. Her last step was to bend the poison out of herself. She had to let go of her fear of the fight that poisoned her. Once the poison was out, her body felt safe and stable again. She even mentioned how her body felt lighter. She had finished the first phase and was ready to start processing what had happened to her.

For you, this phase could look a different way. Find the support you need, the help you need, the environment, and anything else to help your mind and body feel safe. Korra at times tried to jump in too quickly and was overwhelmed and sent back to where she was before.

When she sparred with fire benders, she wasn't ready for a fight and had a flashback of fighting Zahere. Take your time and prepare yourself. There is no rushing this phase. If you take longer than others, it does not mean you are doing something wrong. It means you are doing it exactly right.

<u>Trauma Recovery Phase 2- Remembrance And Mourning</u>

This phase will focus on the remembrance and mourning of the trauma. You will be recalling the trauma more in this phase. The idea is not to relive the trauma. Here is the phase where you will mourn for what happened. It may not be mourning over a lost person or place, it could be the situation in general. To mourn is to experience sorrow or grief. If a situation ends up taking something away from you, you may grieve about the thing or of the lost feeling of safety.

This phase will work best with a professional to help guide you through it. This will help keep the safety and stability you need to complete the healing journey. If by any means you get overwhelmed during this, go back to phase one. Feeling safe will help you control the situation as you go through it. There isn't much direction with this at this point. The therapist or professional you are working with will have the correct direction for your specific situation.

To keep the idea of water bending when you go through this, refer back to Korra's experience. Even though Korra was freer with her body with the poison out and being reunited with her friends, she still had much to process about the trauma. When facing Kuvira soon after her time with Toph, she was met with more flashbacks as she entered the Avatar State. While she could fight much easier, her trauma was still plaguing her mind and keeping her from connecting with Raava. It was time for her to grieve what had happened.

This process was when she went to face Zahere. Her intentions were to look him in the eyes and say that she wasn't scared of him anymore. That quickly failed as Zahere's rush forward her terrified her. This opened the session to begin between them. She let out her anger on how she believed he had ruined her, that she couldn't be the Avatar she should be because of him. Zahere listened and directed her away from that notion because she was still capable. He directed her towards her block from entering the spirit world, even when she's in a place bursting with spiritual energy.

He was able to guide her in a direction she may have been avoiding, a new perspective to show her that her power is limitless and that she can rise up and be the Avatar. Once he knew she was the only one who can undo his actions that led to Kuvira being in charge, he offered to guide her to the spirit world. This action can be seen as her grieving for the events that happened with the support she needed as she went through it. When she started to think she couldn't do it, Zahere was able to remind her that she could, granting her some stability in her effort. With his support, Korra was finally able to enter the Spirit World and reconnect with Raava. Korra was finally able to process what had happened in the way she needed to move past the control it had on her life.

This process could take you a while or not much time at all. It is a matter of who you are and what you need. Korra needed a long time in phase one and a little in phase two. By the time she got to Zahere, she was in a place to be able to fully complete phase two. His support, while you may not find it from your wrongdoer, was the support she needed as she faced her trauma. Sitting through it gave her the acceptance and emotions she needed to get out.

The final phase is like a breath of fresh air. Now, you will reconnect and integrate back into the world. Essentially, this will be you using what you have learned from the experience and putting it into use to better yourself in society. Think of it as you are taking the reins back from someone. You will find there is a multitude you can do here. There is reconnecting with people and communities you distanced yourself from. Bringing your experience into the world to help those in similar situations. New skills will be found in the process which you can use to better your own work. There is no limit to what this could mean for you.

Looking at Korra's journey, we can start by looking at where we last looked at it. She was able to reconnect with Raava, her Avatar spirit. After processing her trauma, Korra was able to accept her role as Avatar again in full commitment. Her fear of her past enemies and what had happened to her had become a lesson now. She learned from her past enemies in a few ways where she was aware that they didn't necessarily have bad values, they were just too extreme with them. The knowledge that she took to the fight against Kuvira.

Korra had also learned that her power is actually limitless after talking with Zahere. The poison should have killed her, yet she was alive. This knowledge can be found as she fights Kuvira, when the spirit beam was accidentally pointed at them and about to shoot them, Korra no longer feared she may be too weak, she had faith her power could help save them both from the beam. This ultimately saved both their lives.

Korra felt more confident than ever in her power, she looked at opposing sides differently and even developed a bit more compassion. She was the Avatar again with more experience. Look for the ways your experiences and lessons can help others and yourself in your Avatarhood.

Korra: "What am I going to find if I get through this?"
Katara: "I don't know, but won't it be interesting to find out?"

A journey of healing yourself from a traumatic experience has no guaranteed ending to look forward to. Katara mentioned Aang's outcome from his traumatic experience of losing his entire culture. For Aang, he found the meaning in his suffering. The meaning is up to him, though you can imagine it was full of compassion and love for others, bringing a new sense of being the Avatar to the world and reconstructing his nation into existence again. What we do know for sure is that it brought him peace. The journey to heal from the experience brought him something other than grief, anger, and depression. Korra faces this mystery not expecting the same outcome Aang got. She understood enough that there is comfort in not being alone with Aang's story, but there was no guarantee they would have the same outcome. Choosing to go on the journey isn't set in stone; you won't be X, Y, and Z at the end. Many times you will find different things about yourself than you thought before. Embrace the mystery and see what's on the other side of the journey for you. Life has a funny way of going the right direction, the one that you truly need when you walk the path with the full determination to get past all of it.

<u>Forgiveness</u>

When Katara returned from her field trip with Zuko to confront the man who murdered her mother in the episode *The Southern Raiders*, Aang greeted them and responded with "forgiveness is the first step you have to take to begin healing." To Katara, forgiveness meant something different than the normal sense of the word that many interpret it as. In many cases, forgiveness is seen as an act of giving an ok to the act that wronged you. Almost like the person is being pardoned for their crimes. This is not the truest form of the word. Forgiveness is the act of choosing to release feelings of resentment and vengeance. It is not to excuse the wrongdoings of those who have harmed you, rather you are choosing to not continue your grudge against them.

It can be a lot to take in when thinking about what the true meaning of forgiveness is. In the end, it is not a pardon at all to the party in the wrong, instead, it is yourself choosing to not carry the overwhelming emotions of anger and resentment towards them. You can still hold the belief that there is no excuse for what they did, you are only letting go of the negative energy that you have been carrying which was caused by their actions. This is a step to heal yourself, not to help them clear their conscience.

Katara, while she said she will never forgive the man who murdered her mother, actually did do the act of forgiveness. She was set on revenge when she went to face him but she let him go. This is the moment of forgiveness. Katara had finally let her feeling of vengeance go. There was no more drive after the release of anger towards him. Her resentment for the Fire Nation crumbled as she then let Zuko into her life. The boundary her resentment made was then taken down.

This is what is meant when people say to forgive someone. Let out the negative raw emotion for good. Allow yourself to connect with people again, to heal your soul again. Forgiveness is to help you, never the party in the wrong. Forgiveness holds a false connotation, leading people to think they must surrender themselves to the acts that wronged them. Often not releasing the true emotion that lingers in them.

In your life, there may be people or groups you would benefit from forgiving. The events that hurt you may still boil within you when you think about it. You still wish justice on them more than wishing the things you want to go right in your life. You crave vengeance, a taste of their own medicine. Hoping that karma shows its face and grants everything you've imagined to them. Resentment still rests within you. You do not have to pardon what they did, they don't deserve that. What you deserve, though, is to be released from those feelings. To allow the positive energy to flow through you again. It is time you choose true forgiveness.

The action of forgiving does not have to be as extravagant as is seen with Katara. Going up to your wrongdoer and nearly murdering them may worsen your position, if not internally, then definitely legally. Many times you may not even get the reaction out of them if you just yell at them, giving you no release but instead creating more anger inside you. The reaction you want will never be guaranteed if you confront the wrongdoer. Think of when Korra went to confront Zahere and instead of repentance, he terrified her by making a rushing motion towards her. There is no way to know how someone will react.

Find methods that will be a controlled environment to release it, where you are not reliant on someone else's response. Writing out what you would say to them on paper could work. Instead of actually delivering it to them to read, burn it, tear it up, destroy it any way you can. In the letter, you can even talk about how you forgive them only for yourself, that they are not worth your energy and that there is still no excuse for what was done. Closing with that may be the last bit of energy you need to release from yourself. Then let it go with the destruction of the paper. If you give it to them, just know you will most likely not get the response you want from them.

It may all fade there, though you may also feel the resentment still linger after. As people of habit, shaking emotions can be hard to shake off. Revisit your forgiveness in your meditation. Use mala beads to reaffirm that you will not hold on to those feelings. Affirmations where you are empowering your healing journey from them may also work. The idea is to create a new habit in your emotions.

Once you have reached true forgiveness, look to reconnect to those around you. In times of pain, it is easy to distance ourselves and to push your unwanted feelings onto others. You do not have to reconnect with the wrongdoer. Through mutual connections may have been affected. To restore things you will have to take action in reaching out to them. If you are having trouble wanting to, see if there is more resentment and vengeance within you at their possible involvement. Once you have cleared yourself from these feelings, you will become in control again.

When you have reached the point of true forgiveness, do not think you can never remember what happened. You can still remember. You are only dealing with the negative feelings that plague you, halting your progression in your healing process and journey in life. It will take time to get to this point, but you can reach it and the clear mind from it that you deserve.

<u>Movement</u>

The style of water bending used by the water tribes is based on real-world martial arts known as Tai Chi. This ancient tradition not only provides defense in combat but also provides health and wellbeing in its movement. Think of it as a saying you've probably heard before, "use it or lose it." As you go about your life and stop using your body in a certain aspect, the body will adapt to save strength and energy by releasing the ability to do so. This is why after your leg has been in a cast, it needs to go through physical therapy. The muscle deteriorates and no longer can fulfill the task they were once able to do so easily.

In today's world, there is an epidemic of screens that leads people to live sedentary lifestyles. Computers have opened a new world of thousands of new jobs that can be done all as a desk. Sitting for eight hours a day plus then going home to relax on your couch to watch TV, play video games or play on your phone- not to mention the amount of time sitting while driving between those- has created a sedentary lifestyle for many. The body was never designed to do this, as you can imagine it hasn't even been a century where people have had easy access to the internet or even a computer at all. Television wasn't even invented until 1927, again not even a century as of writing this book. There were not many leading humans to a sedentary life.

Our bodies were instead programmed to be able to do things such as hunting and gathering to survive. Being able to run to escape predators. Bending down had less strain on the back as people did it so often to pick their harvest. People were designed to survive just as animals in the wild are. A physically capable body is what you may have experienced as a child. Being able to run around for hours, climb into small low down places, be able to take a fall, and much more. The body was trained to do that and kept up with it. This is why you were able to keep doing it as a kid. Once you started to do less, maybe watching television more often, your body started to adapt to that. If it wasn't going to undergo the strenuous labors you put it through as a child, then why would it perform the maintenance needed on the body? On the couch, you didn't need that.

It's very similar to how you become rusty at something after not doing it for so long. For instance, let's say you go to play basketball after years of not even stepping on a court. While you may have been able to make a dozen shots with no problem before, now you seem to miss the majority of them. The body had no reason to keep that skill as it wasn't being used, so it put it to the forgotten side and moved on with the skills you were using. This can go further than just the physical act of doing something. Think of the organs that work when you are moving. The heart pumps your blood as you take in more oxygen as you exert yourself. When you are out of practice, so is your heart. This is how you seem to always be out of breath.

At this point, you may be fearing that you have to start running five miles a day or something. Not necessarily. The idea though is to incorporate more movement into your body. This can be done in many different ways, and it will be up to you to see what combination will work best for your lifestyle. There will be a talk about regular exercise in the coming pages, though there will also be a talk of normal everyday movement that can do wonders as well.

To get it out of the way, let's talk about exercise. This doesn't have to be a hardcore everyday type of exercise. Two to three days a week would be fine if you do it correctly. Look into the different types of exercise and find one that you enjoy. You could enjoy running and set aside a couple of days to go run at least a mile or so. Or you could partake in other forms of cardio. Biking can be a fun way to cruise around your neighborhood or nature. The main idea is to move, control your breathing as you go, and make sure the body uses those muscles that get neglected when you're sitting down.

There is also strength training. This form doesn't mean you will become a bodybuilder. Just because you bench press a couple of times doesn't mean you'll look like The Boulder. Instead, a couple of times a week can really help keep your body capable of the movement you would be ignoring otherwise. Within this type of exercise, you will be tailoring your workout to your goals. If you do not want to become muscular, don't worry, that won't happen unless you mean for it to happen. This method has tremendous effects on the heart, joints, and overall health. This can be done at a gym with loads of equipment or a couple of dumbbells at home, it has a very wide range of possibilities. Look into it if you feel this might be a good choice for you and make sure to find a plan that has your goals in mind.

There are more forms of exercises than just those two, those are just two of the top practiced ones. There are many different ways you can pick up a workout such as Zumba, CrossFit, walking, sports, or even a martial arts class. Tai Chi would be the more ironic one to choose for this, though there is much truth behind why it is the source form of water bending. It is a low-impact movement that can be taken very slowly. Think of yourself as moving like water during it, yet you will still come out with sweat and sore legs.

Beyond a few hours in a week to focus on just exercise and its movements, take a look at how you can become less sedentary in your daily life. If you are sitting at work or at home, you can try to get up and walk around a little every hour. This will increase the blood flow, causing you to think more sharply. Not only that, but you will be making sure it moves more in general. This can go a long way compared to the amount of movement it gets from just sitting, and the reach to grab the remote does not count.

The importance of blood flow is a matter of how well your body can heal itself when it needs to. When you move, your blood will get more oxygen which it sends to the rest of the body. That nutrient can then help the body stay healthy and repair itself when needed. This is why after surgery and other procedures, doctors try to make sure you at least get up to walk a little. There is a lot of reasons that are important after a medical procedure, including preventing blood clots, but in the end, it's all geared towards your health, not because they want to torture you.

Earlier it was only mentioned that walking can be a form of exercise to help you with this, and it's true. Walking a simple walk in a day can do much with the body's health that has been already mentioned. The benefits go beyond physical health as you will find your mind clearer. Getting out of a stale environment can recharge it, take in the sights and sounds, let your battery recharge like one of those cars you pull back and it flings it forward. If you don't want to walk outside, go to the mall and walk. People and nature watch as you walk. If you have a dog, take him for more walks in the park. Move your body, it doesn't have to be a huge production, just enough so you don't lose it.

<u>Mindfulness</u>

One of the most underrated and least taken care of organs in our body is the brain. Our mind is reliant on this organ to function. In today's world, it is found that the stigma of getting help for our mental wellbeing hurts many that need it. Much of this may not be seen, though there is still great harm that comes to us if our mind is not taken care of. Instead of going into more on how to seek help, as it was already covered, let's look into more of a daily practice you can do for mindfulness.

Mindfulness is essentially being aware and conscious of something. It may seem familiar to your air bending training, though it goes much deeper than that. This act can help to increase our ability to regulate emotions, decrease stress, anxiety, and depression. Essentially, mindfulness is a tool you can use to battle against these. We have touched a bit on the other benefits such as focusing our attention back with air bending, though there are parts of it we can still use now. To be able to focus and notice our feelings and emotions without judgment can be a big part of changing the narrative of mental stresses.

Meditation is a common tool for practicing this. The focus on the breath and letting your mind wander without becoming upset is essentially what mindfulness is about. There isn't much more to add to your meditation than what you already know.

Noticing will be the big focal point in this training. Noticing is one thing our mind does without even thinking about noticing. Sometimes you just notice someone got a haircut when you weren't even thinking about it. Now, you will notice on purpose. To begin, let's look at how Katara in the episode *The Waterbending Scroll* teaches water bending to Aang. She describes the flow of the water to him, being present and finding the details within it. Katara also mentions how to feel the energy of the moon at night. These are the small things that happen as a bender, though it is up to you to focus on putting the attention on them.

Start this practice by noticing the movements you already make in your daily life. Describe them in your head. The feeling, speed, strength, and anything you can think of. This will be going beyond being an observer from your air bending training. In that training, you were focused on the world around you, here you will focus more on yourself. This will open up the details of yourself to yourself. Not like looking in a mirror and noticing details, but noticing details in the energy and strength of your body.

Your next water bending exercise here will be to only do one thing at a time. Remember how chaotic Korra's life was when she juggled airbending practice, pro-bending, and hunting Amon? She was everywhere, emotions heightened, and wasn't accomplishing anything. Once pro-bending was done and her air bending training put on hold, she was able to take down Amon. This lesson should be taken seriously in your own life. Multitasking does not exist. You are simply breaking your focus each time you go to the next thing. Focusing on one thing at a time will allow you to fully see what you're doing and complete it in a quicker manner with higher satisfaction.

Multitasking isn't just with immediate tasks, such as cooking dinner while doing dishes and helping someone with their homework. That multitasking is also toxic to your mindfulness, but so is it on a bigger picture. Let's say you are going to school, have a job, writing a book, and are taking care of a family. While it may be hard to get out of those situations, it is still a multitasking scenario on a bigger scale. You are so tied between these things that you can't dedicate yourself to the time needed at just one. Oftentimes you will see one get lost on the way, maybe in this case the writing of a book and even the schooling. Slow down if you can and find people to help you. If this is on another scale such as you are writing a book, writing a play, acting in a play, and learning guitar, drop three and keep the one for now until that is complete. If your mind is on one thing, then you can see the small details and complete it in a mindful way. When it just gets slapped together, you are not being mindful of it.

It will be easier to practice this on a smaller scale at first. Bring all your attention to one task at a time. This will give you time to notice everything going on in the task. You will be concentrated enough to make sure it is done to ultimate satisfaction. You will be practicing focus. You will also be less overwhelmed. When you are overwhelmed, you are trying to look at too many things at once. There is no detail noticing. To deepen the connection of focus on what is in front of you or yourself. If you become overwhelmed, then you have failed to notice how you feel on the way there to be able to step back and control the situation.

Take time to stop and notice yourself, your wellbeing, and your current state. Put down the phone and all other screens and just be with yourself. Be with the small tasks such as taking out the trash. Be aware of yourself and take action when you feel yourself going off course. Meditate and do your water bending training to full mastery. Avatars cannot do everything by themselves, they are human too. Take the time needed to take care of that side of you.

Physical Wounds

. It is important to know how to deal with physical wounds as well. This will help you understand your body as you recover from any physical wound you have. Before getting into the deep end of the topic, know that the first thing you should always do is to listen and follow your doctor's instructions. They are specialists that have trained hard to help you. They will know all the technical things you will need to be good as new.

Now, imagine Korra fighting through her paralysis in her legs. Katara could not simply just heal her legs to work, there was an aspect that was all Korra. Your body will not get better if you choose to not get better. What you think, do, and feel will all affect the outcome of physical wound recovery. When Korra sat in the healing tub, she was frustrated by her lack of movement. Katara told her to concentrate on moving just her big toe. After increased focus and determination, Korra was able to move it.

In your experience, physical wounds may not work out as simple as that. Though it has been shown that the power of vision and focus can speed up the healing process. In the book *Zen in the Martial Arts,* there is a story about karate instructor, Sam Brodsky where he gave a demonstration, resulting in him breaking many small bones in his hand. He had it operated on and told that it would take at least a year for even partial use of his hand again. Brodsky believed that healing was primarily in the mind. Every night when he went to bed, he would imagine tiny men in hard hats coming to work on his hand with all sorts of different tools. In a matter of ten weeks when the doctor looked at it, he called it a miracle. In a matter of ten weeks, the hand was back to functioning instead of the projected year from the doctor. This is the power of visualization.

If the mind is focused on the healing of an injury, then its efforts will be sent there. If the mind is focused on things you wish you could do, stresses of life, or anything else, then the energy will go towards that. Korra's first steps after being paralyzed were this practice as well. Katara told Korra to imagine walking to Nagga. The focus of that image brought Korra to take the few steps needed to reach her friend.

You may not have something as extreme as a broken hand or paralyzed legs, but at times you probably have some medical issue come up. Take getting the flu for instance. Next time you catch this, take time to imagine your body destroying the germs, clear your nostrils, to soothe your throat. Being sick seems to drag on and on when you keep thinking about how you're sick and can't go do what you want to do. See how your body functions with the visualization. Lay in bed before you fall asleep and imagine your body going out to fight the enemy germs that are in your body. Focus your energy on the actions and outcomes of your healing.

Taking care of your body in the basic ways will help give it the strength it needs to heal. Eat only food that gives you the nutrients you need and drink plenty of water. Having your body stressed over lack of these necessities will only harm progress. Also, get plenty of rest when you need it. The body can do most of its healing when you rest. It's not trying to do as many things as you go about your day and think about hot topics at the moment. It needs to focus as much energy as it can on the injury, and as we learned earlier, multitasking doesn't work.

<u>Bringing It All together</u>

Once you have grasped your waterbending abilities and are confident in them, it is time to put them to the test. Throughout your own process, you probably intertwined the techniques and philosophies as you sought out the right path for you. From here you can use these skills for further injury or illness that becomes upon you. These will be timeless as you face hardships in your life. Never hesitate to revisit this section if you feel you need guidance in healing yourself.

You now can use these tools to help others as well. Not in a sense a doctor or therapist would unless you are licensed to do so. But in ways to help support those around you. Many times, people feel lost and uncertain of their next steps. With your help, you can help bring them peace of mind and the guidance needed to find the right people to work with. Share with them your own experiences and what has worked for you. Share the book if you have to. The idea is to have the information they need and give it to them.

Think of yourself as a healer as great as Katara. Katara is very skilled. Katara also understands that the best thing to help people heal is to bring guidance to people to help them find their own way. Listen actively and gently push them in the right direction. Let those around you share their emotions and feelings like they are pouring water out of a bucket.

Like it has been said before, there is no one right way to go about any of this. Sometimes you might mess up, though, by the end of your training, you will feel much more confident in helping those around you. Everyday try to strive to help those facing their traumas, injuries, and illnesses. Katara never deserted people who needed help. That mentality is one of a true water bender. They are caring and nurturing. If they need to step in and help, they will do so. When people in the Avatar universe are hurt badly, they recommend going to the North Pole for healers or Katara in the South Pole. They are the best at what they do because they dedicate themselves to it. Now it is time for you to do the same.

Uncle Iroh's Wisdom

"Sometimes the best way to solve your own problems is to help someone else."

You would be surprised what can happen from helping others. Doors become unlocked for you, joyful emotions happen and you learn from another experience. This isn't to say that you should only help others to help yourself, but be open to the idea that it could help you in the long run. If you are stuck on something, don't use that as an excuse to only think about that and turn down helping someone in need. Instead, take time off the problem and help them. You may find your mind opens up and the answers you've been looking for are all right there. You can even find fulfillment in a problem by redeeming yourself by helping others. Many emotions can make you feel lost, the power of helping others is a solution to become unlost.

The Healing Element

Healing is a skill water benders hold proudly when they are capable of doing it. This is the only element that can directly fix the human body as they use water to repair the tissue in the body. For you, this is more than fixing physical wounds, but to be there to help someone mend their way when they are hurt. It may be traditional in the Northern Water Tribe to have only women learn this skill, but it is not a requirement here. Instead, everyone can benefit from learning the skill of healing. To be able to support and guide people in the right direction is a high honor that can have a lasting impact on those around you and the injured. The Avatar is gifted the duty to keep balance in the world, healing is part of that. It isn't always about bending fights, even if they are cool to watch. Sometimes it's about listening and other times it's about just focusing on helping someone get better, as we saw many times before from healers.

The Blood Bending Element

This is an element that can be used in a terrible way. It's been seen how gruesome it can be to see people lose control of their bodies, being twisted in all different ways, all against their will. Blood bending is an act of forcing someone to do something, and that is not something you should do. It is possible to help guide people, though force will only make them resent you. Like in the series, there hasn't been a positive impact from this sub-bending. It's hard to believe such a cruel act can come from a serene element as water. Instead, focus on making yourself do things. It has been touched on before about volition. Now use your water bending to use volition with more purpose. When you feel the pull away from wanting to help someone, use it to put yourself back on track. As humans, it is possible to resist the right moral thing to do in a situation. This is where you use blood bending on yourself. Force yourself to do what you don't want to because you know it's the right thing.

How You Will Know You Are Ready

Like before when you evaluated yourself after learning Earth, Fire, and Air, you will be scoring yourself to see your mastery of Water. As before, here is a checklist to measure where you are. Each item should be scored on a 1-10 rating. 1 is the lowest indicating that you have nothing and have only read the section. 10 will be the highest and means you are confident in the work you have done in that section and see no more need to improve it. Add up the scores at the end and look at your overall score. Think of it as a letter grade in school, 90-100 is an A, 80-89 is a B, 70-79 is a C, 60-69 is a D and everything below that is an F. The goal here is to reach for an A. While other scores are considered passing, they don't indicate mastery. You could move on in the average level grades such as B and C, but be aware that your healing power is only as powerful as you make it.

___You have fully accepted the healing process.

___You have sought out the specialized help you will need on
        your journey.
___You understand phase 1 and are creating safety and
        stabilization.
___You understand phase 2 and are willing to follow a
        professional in the field you need to process and grieve.
___You understand phase 3 and will use this phase to use your
        new experiences and lessons to integrate fully back into
society.
___You understand and have made significant progress on
forgiveness towards those who have wronged you.
___You have implemented movement into your daily life.

___You have gained control over mindfulness.

___You understand and are capable of using visualization to help
your injuries and illnesses heal.
___You feel confident that you can use all these skills to help
        others in need.
____ Overall score

Non- Bender Friends

Why We Must Learn From Non-benders

The four elements give you powers beyond any normal person. Yet, we see time after time where non-benders end up triumphing over benders. Sokka took out Combustion Man with his boomerang. Asami took down Red Lotus guards to rescue the Air Nomads and Korra. Suki fought through fire benders to reach the Boiling Rock warden, taking him hostage. Mai standing up to Azula with Ty Lee then chi blocking Azula. Time and time again it has been proven that there is more than bending to win a fight.

As the Avatar, it is important to incorporate all wisdom from everywhere you go. There is no avoiding non-benders, as they intermingle in the grand scheme of life in the world. Working with the lessons and skills that they hold will unlock possibilities you may not have thought of before. Remember that it was non-benders who progressed the world technologically. You have the Mechanist with all of his inventions that made life unique to the people who inhabited the Northern Air Temple. The Satomobile and other mechs and planes were made by Hiroshi Sato. Even Sokka with his idea for the submarine. Without bending, these people have had to find ways to be just as capable in the world as a bender, often leading to inventions that leveled the playing field.

Understanding may even help defuse rifts between the two. We see in the *Legend of Korra* the rise of Equalist and in *the Last Airbender* comics the feuds that rose within the rise of factories such as Earthen Fire. Each time the Avatar stepped in to bring balance to the situation the best they could. While it may not have gone as smoothly as they were hoping at first, they had the heart to know that non-benders are just as entitled to things as benders are. In your own life, you may be able to use these skills to be able to help rifts between others as well. With so many walks of life, there are plenty of disagreements that come about. It is a matter of being an unbiased third party to help communication happen.

As you go through this section, don't think you can skip out on the exercises and be the best Avatar ever. Take them as seriously as you did your element training. It may not be as flashy as the past training or skills, though there is a lot of skill to be learned. Remember these are skills of those who help push the world forward without any elemental help. Mixing what you learn here with what you already know will only make you stronger and wiser.

Uncle Iroh's Wisdom

"It is important to draw wisdom from different places. If you take it from only one place, it becomes rigid and stale."

By looking at all people, cultures, and ways of life, you will see that there is more solution to a problem. Take in everything you can and learn from everyone, this will give you more knowledge than is

---

> needed to solve problems. This will make solutions more well-rounded as you take into consideration all of them.

Characteristics Of Non- Benders

When looking at the character of a non- bender, you see many different varieties. Non-benders live amongst all the nations, bringing with them those cultures as well. The difference is that they don't have the influence of the element. We see Bumi before he became an air bender, uninfluenced by the elements even though he was raised by a water bender and an air bender, who was the Avatar. Bumi steered his thought process in a different direction than his siblings. Bumi wanted to help the world, though there was no calling to healing or to restoring the Air Nation. Instead, he joined the United Forces, developing his own military esque ways.

Not to mention those who were fully immersed in the culture all their lives also strayed from the elemental side. Sokka called Katara's water bending weird and magic. He had no intention of learning about it or how bending influences their culture. Each time Katara would mention it was a part of their culture he blew it off for more pressing matters such as food or protecting his home.

On the flip side, there are non-benders that don't link to any of the cultures, Asami and her father, Hiroshi Sato. This family has no ties to the elements. They were born in the United Republic, giving them no elemental bias in their culture. There was so much of a separation that Hiroshi absolutely loathed benders all together due to the accident that killed his wife. You can see much success in the family nonetheless. Hiroshi Sato built an empire for himself by creating the

Satomobile and Asami has proven herself as a businesswoman running the company as well as handling herself in a tussle with thugs.

There are some traits that can be seen as mutual between many of the non-benders. During the Last Airbender, many of them were equipped with fantastic weapon skills, strategic planning, improvisation, and bravery. Hearing those words, characters such as Sokka, Suki, Mai, and Ty Lee may have come to mind. Furthering these traits in the *Legend of Korra* you may think of creative, confident, skilled combat, intelligent, leadership and even crazy. Characters you may have thought of may have been Asami, Hiroshi, Varrick, Baatar jr., and Bumi. All of these characters made a significant impact on the world in their own ways using these characteristics.

You may be wondering how you will make use of all these traits. You can't necessarily make yourself all of that, and why would you need to become them when many of these things come from your previous training. The thing is, most of this has been talked about in some ways. The reason you need to revisit these things in the eyes of a non-bender is so you can see the many different ways you can utilize your Avatar skills.

<u>Knowing Your Own Power</u>

One of the marvelous things about non-benders is that they don't stew over the fact that they can't manipulate the elements. Benders make comments on how they don't know how to go on if they don't have their bending, not seeing how people can survive without it. It is their identity. You never hear non-benders complaining about it though. This lesson can teach you a couple of different things. One is that you need to own your own power, even if it's not bending. The second is to not complain about what life has dealt you.

Looking at the first lesson, look at the non-benders and what each one brings to the table. Sokka is skilled with his boomerang, sword, and strategic plan-making. Suki is a highly skilled warrior in hand-to-hand combat as well as fan weaponry. Ty Lee learned chi blocking while Mai throws knives. Asami has a taser glove and combat training while also using her intelligence in running a major company. Varrick can come up with crazy inventions and plans to get him out of trouble. Bumi is a highly skilled commander with all the skills that it requires. None of them are exactly the same in terms of skill. Looking at benders, air bending is about the same as any other air bending. The same with the other elements, they all just move that one element.

Each skill has proven itself against a bender in some way or another. They learned to master their talents and skills and use them in situations to get an edge. There is no moping about how they want bending, instead, they confidently use their own skills to get the job done. Suki during the riot at the Boiling Rock threw herself into the chaos to run over the fire-spewing benders to parkour her way up the tower to take the warden hostage. At this time, she did not have any of her armor or fans. She knew that she had other skills beyond her uniform and weapon and flung herself without warning out into the danger. She managed to capture the warden without any trouble and got him to the trolly to escape with. With no hesitation, she used her skills in the presence of not just bending, but chaotic bending that went everywhere around and at her.

The confidence in their own skills made the benders they worked alongside also respect them. When Team Avatar was in need of a plan, they turned to Sokka, the idea guy. In the comic *Imbalance,* to help the non-bender guards they all turned to Suki and her expertise. Azula had no problem giving tasks to Mai and Ty Lee as she knew they were fully capable of going up against any bender. Bolin even turned to Varrik when he needed to escape his crazy girlfriend, Eska. When you show what your skills can do and do it with confidence, those around you will call on you when they need help. It isn't a world where benders only can help non-benders. Non-benders have their place in everything too as they come to the aid of their friends and allies.

The second lesson is one that can slip people's minds easily, and that is gratitude. As mentioned before, non-benders do not complain about not being benders. They understand very quickly that it was not in the cards for them. This opens their mind to everything around them. They pick up multiple skills along the way instead of just honing the one. Sokka was a trained warrior with a boomerang at the beginning of the series. He showed no interest in the fact that his sister could bend, and throughout the series, he did not express jealousy towards those who could. Sokka had other skills such as strategic planning, observance, and leadership. He didn't stop there in his journey. When they were hiding out in the Fire Nation, Sokka found Master Piandao and learned how to fight with a sword. Weaponry has many different categories, though lots of them won't transfer into each other. A boomerang and club are very different from handling a sword. It's not like learning a sub bending, it's learning an entirely new element.

You Are Everyone's Avatar

In the Legend of Korra episode *When Extremes Meet,* there is a scene where Tarlock is enforcing a non-bender curfew with the police force. In the chaos of the non-benders being bound by metal, one calls out to Korra for help and states "You're our Avatar too." It can be hard to imagine that someone in charge of so much power and keeping the world in balance would also represent those without bending. This goes back to why it's important to understand these people, or else you cannot represent and help them.

While this doesn't directly relate to a trait or skill non-benders have, it's a great reminder this Republic City citizen gave. Aang and Korra both had close friends that were non-benders. The Avatar's friends are very important in the influence of the Avatar to help guide them through grey areas in life. Sokka helped Aang many times by bringing his own perspective to things in the comic *Imbalance*. He gave insight as a non-bender looking at the feud between the benders and non-benders in the town. This not only gave a voice for the non-benders but helped show the Avatar their side of the story.

Learn the wisdom of non-benders, especially if they are involved in the subject. In your life, think of those who may not identify as the same as you. Help understand their communities and beliefs. For example, if you are not a member of the LGBT+ community, try reaching out to those who are for the perspective and knowledge on issues within that community. Oftentimes when we try to make the world a better place, we can forget those who may not exactly benefit like we hope in certain efforts. Talk to them and understand them. This will bring more insight into how the world works beyond just your bender friends.

Even on the side of keeping people safe from wrongdoings of non-benders is always part of the job. Hiroshi Sato in the first book of Legend of Korra, shadowed by Amon's lead in the equalist movement, was a major benefactor in the cause. He supplied equipment for the non-benders including their tasing gloves and mech suits. Before it was known, Korra had her suspicions after overhearing him talking on the phone. She took this situation as seriously as she did Amon.

You are connected to non-benders no matter what. Whatever you do will affect them in a way too, but it might not always be a positive outcome if you don't think about it. Strive to help all people no matter their differences. If you find one being truly threatening, do what you can to defuse the situation and help those that are hurt by their actions. You are everyone's Avatar after all.

<u>Being Resourceful</u>

One thing you can always count on from non-benders is being resourceful. In battle, they are observant of their surroundings. It was part of Sokka's sword training where he had to take in his entire surroundings in a few seconds and then draw it from memory. This skill gives the non-bender a sense of advantage as they can pinpoint danger spots and plan new strategies. After training with Master Paindoa with a sword, we see Sokka having to fight him off to prove he has mastered it. During the fight, we hear Paindoa comment on how Sokka's use of his surroundings is excellent as he used them to avoid attacks and set himself up for his own attacks.

While you won't be using this in combat and this may seem a little bit like your Air bending training, think of it as taking your observer skills to the next level. Now, you will be finding things around you to use at a moment's notice. Think about when you are in a meeting with someone and you need to convince them of your idea. There is rehearsing involved, yes. But there are also many advantages to looking around their office when you go there and making conversation on something. This will make them feel happy and proud to share their knowledge and accomplishments with you. This could also help you notice something that you may have in your presentation but could damage getting them on your side. Think about sports, if you have a comment planned about a team that won over the weekend, you may find that the team that lost against them is decorated inside the person's office. Bringing up the disappointment may harsh their mood and become less likely to buy the idea.

You may also find that finding the right people can get you into the door. Take Asami for instance, she had a meeting planned with Varrick for a partnership at the beginning of the Spirits Festival in episode *Rebel Spirit*. She decided to bring Bolin to stand in as an assistant, to help her look more professional. Bolin was a key to getting Varrick more interested in Sato Industries. When Bolin pointed out that Varrick wasn't in fact floating at all, Varrick knew instantly that these were people she wanted to work with. Asami's attention to small details on having an assistant lead to her partnership with Varrick. Not to mention Varrick has his handful of resourcefulness as he is famous for hiding in a platypus bear and spewing money from the butt as a distraction to escape onto a boat.

Look for the small things to add to an appearance. Even adding a partner to stand by when you have meetings, will be able to also help find the do's and don'ts of the place. Or you may find that you can use the person you brought to your advantage so you may give your full attention to the person you are talking to while they do any handling of presentation material. There are numerous ways you can be resourceful in any situation. Even simply bringing coffee because it's an early morning meeting can make a difference.

This can also be done in your own office by setting the room up in certain ways. Yale did a study in 2008 to see if certain temperatures would affect people's decisions. In the study, they would ask

176

participants to hold a hot or cold therapeutic pad for a product evaluation study. After, they would offer them a gift certificate they could give to a friend or a gift they could keep themselves. The ones that had the hot therapeutic pad tended to choose the certificate for a friend while those who held the cold tended to choose the gift for themselves. This study can be useful in your resourcefulness by focusing on how to make an environment and yourself warmer to get the yes you want. This shows that a warm setting will bring a person to say yes more easily versus the feeling of being cold. Find colors and other manipulations to make the room feel warmer in all aspects to influence the people you need to succeed.

The objective is to find the solutions around you to succeed in the conflict in front of you. Think of Varrick choosing money to distract people away from what he was trying to do while in the platypus bear suit. Go about situations with the resourcefulness you need to set up all environmental factors to your advantage.

Uncle Iroh's Wisdom

"The only thing better than finding something you are looking for is finding something you weren't looking for at a great bargain!"

A play on the idea of finding something you weren't looking for being the thing that you need. While Iroh didn't need all the treasures from the pirate's shop, he still found happiness in the discovery. You never know what you might find in life. You could be looking for something and find something completely different and realize that it's what you actually needed all along. Take these gifts life will throw your way. You may find that there are a whole bunch of things you needed all along.

<u>Being Strategic</u>

The first non-bender that comes to mind when thinking of strategic planning would have to be Sokka. This Water Tribe non-bender was trained to be able to protect a village alone while the men of the tribe were away. He was put in charge of teaching the young children how to protect the village. When he left with Aang and Katara, he was the one they would turn to to get a plan. Sokka was even the mastermind of the invasion plan for the Day of Black Sun.

Being strategic will be different from being resourceful, as this will be the preplanning. Sokka is a well-versed non-bender in this scenario as he is the "idea guy". Before, it has been said over and over again to plan ahead of things. Know what paths and tasks you need to take in your journey. Sokka does this on the next level. He is able to plan ahead while in a tough situation that didn't go according to prior plan. Think about when he was inside the drill trying to break into Ba Sing Se. He already knew going in blind was a bad idea, so as soon as they infiltrated, he made sure to snag a map from an engineer. With the map, he was able to plan the rest of the attack quickly as he determined the braces are what hold it all together. He guided Aang and Katara to the braces and told them to use water bending to cut through the metal. What to take away from this is that no matter how much of a rush you are in, slow down to get the correct plans. If Sokka didn't plan to lure an engineer to get the map, they would have been aimlessly trying to take it down by attacking random structures. This led them straight to the workings that mattered most.

You may find you are on a deadline at some point and are running out of time. Something may not have gone to plan and now you are scrambling to get it all together. Stepping back to look at the big picture and evaluate what needs to be done can cut off time you would have been wasting doing things blindly. If you are trying to memorize a script for a play, you may feel the heat of a deadline to know them. Instead of just trying to learn it all in order and going through everything every time you go to practice, look through for the hardest parts and prioritize them until they are down pat. This will make the overwhelming task of learning all those lines seem manageable. Planning ahead, even when you feel like you need to rush, will give you the time you need.

Looking closer to Sokka's methods of strategic planning, you can see where he finds an opportunity whenever he can to learn more about his opponent. While Team Avatar was taking mini-vacations in season two, Sokka chose his vacation to find a way to take down the Fire Nation. He chose to visit Wan Shi Tong's Spirit Library for the sheer purpose of finding dirt on the Fire Nation. Even when he's relaxing, he's keeping an eye out for possibilities. While at the Library we see him risk as much time as he can to figure out the exact date of the eclipse so he may give the information to the Earth King. Then when Ba Sing Se is taken over and the Earth Kingdom can no longer use its army against the Fire Nation, Sokka takes it into his own hands to use the information to still go through with a plan and take down the Fire Lord.

Use every opportunity to find something useful to help yourself. This may be finding a book that can help you find answers or it could be getting information second-hand from someone you've just met. Even if you are on a trip for business and you learn about a place that has to do with something else you are interested in, find time to go there. That is where you find your greatest finds. This can also help by going to events you know nothing about. If you are in business and see a lecture on solar energy, who is to say that that information can't help you in some way. There is information everywhere, you just need to focus on getting it.

<u>Showing No Fear</u>

In the episode *The Avatar Returns* in the Last Airbender, we see Zuko's ship enter the village walls and Sokka is the only one-armed to protect everyone. Sokka attacks with his club and boomerang and fails. Then a small Water Tribe child tosses him a spear and chants "Show no fear." This is essential for a non-bender. If they show their fear then the foundation will crack. Benders will lose all caution towards them. This is why Sokka always boldly goes forth when in a fight.

Non-benders that end up in combat have a tendency to have a very stoic expression as they mask any fear or nerves they may be feeling. They know they are capable, but it's hard to always be confident when you have fire being hurled at you. Even with that kind of threat, we see many of them step up to the plate and deliver. Think of Suki when she and the Kyoshi warriors found Appa alone. Azula found him and threatened all of them, though Suki never hesitated a bit at the thought of a battle with the fire bender. She put on her brave face and made sure Appa escaped, ultimately leading to her capture. She would have had a better chance if she escaped right away, but that wasn't an option. She risked the chance of being captured.

Don't run into a fight to practice controlling your fear. That would be a gruesome way to grow as a person who wants to better the world. Instead, practice by doing things that already scare you. It may be public speaking or wearing a shirt with something unusual on it in public. Only you know your fears. Though instead of trying to get over those fears, focus on not showing you are nervous and scared. This could over time help you get over the fear of that thing, but it will prepare you when you know you need to stand your ground on something.

Asami grew up in a wealthy, protected home where she could do most of what she pleases. She was taught self-defense as a safety precaution and nothing else. Once she found out about her father helping the equalist, she looked confused before she went into a confident face once she put on the gloves. That is when Hiroshi had his guard down and she took it to tase him. Hiding the fear made it possible for her to save her friends, even though she felt so much emotion going against her father like she did.

This does not mean to deceit people to get what you want, in a way. Instead, take from it the power of a non-fear filled face. It will help people bring down their guard, maybe even enough for you to be able to help. It's hard to help those with their guard up. They are skeptical, and if you show fear or hesitancy, they usually retreat more into what they are hiding behind. Take this opportunity to find out how to help instead of them dodging the question.

You could also use this when confronting people. If they see fear then they know that they can find and break your root. But if you keep up the brave face they won't see the opening. This will open the opportunity to talk to them and find the solution. Those who can find a way to bring you down most likely will, that's why you shouldn't leave an opening for them. Make sure you let them know you have purpose and no fear when confronting them.

<u>Don't Take Everything So Seriously</u>

One of the greatest lessons our non-bending friends can teach us is to not take everything so seriously. Sokka's jokes may come to mind as you think about the classic one-liners he gives such as "Flying kick a pow!" Or the fun Suki has picking on Sokka as she trains him. Ty Lee finds joy in many things, almost always having a smile. Varrick and his eccentric explanations and solutions. Even Asami may come to mind as she occasionally takes tense moments to play with people into thinking she doesn't know something.

It's a breath of fresh air as so many characters are so focused on the task at hand that they forget the power of a smile and a laugh. Take this into your daily life to implement the relaxation of humor. Find moments to throw a joke out there or to notice the funny coincidences. Stress can take a toll on the body, even making you more tired than usual. To let the serotonin run through, you once in a while with some laughter will help break the tension and keep yourself healthy.

Life also doesn't seem to be as enjoyable if you don't express joy. Yes, there are instances where it seems impossible. For instance, losing someone can be very hard. This doesn't mean you have to make a joke about the fact that someone is gone. Instead, take the time to grieve. There are ways throughout it to help lift you up as well, such as remembering a funny or joyful memory of the person. It will help lessen the pain of sadness for a second and help celebrate what was.

Practicing laughter meditation may be a good process for handling life's stressful situations. Laughter meditation is just what it sounds like, it's laughing for a set amount of time essentially. To start, you will stand and relax the body and massage the jaw to help prepare it. Then either stand or sit in a comfortable position and start a soft laugh and go into a belly laugh while trying to find your true laugh. It's ok if it is a forced laugh, you will find it will also benefit you in similar ways. Then sit or lay in silence noticing the thoughts that come to mind. This can bring many benefits such as stress release, feeling lighter, connection with others, and release of strong emotions. A different kind of meditation that will feel less serious than the other forms.

Ironically, don't try to take this too seriously. That would ruin the point. Instead, try to make it a point in the day to remind yourself to relax and laugh a bit. If something goes wrong, try laughing instead of fuming. It will take time to get to a place where you will feel natural and comfortable not stressing over everything, because in the end, it might not be worth the energy to get mad at.

<u>Chi Blocking</u>

Chi blocking was in no doubt a game changer when it was introduced. This skill is one anyone can learn as it is knowing where to jab to render the person in front of you useless. It can work to disable non-benders temporarily, making them lose control of their limbs, but it can do much more to benders. Being able to temporarily take away bending is a major threat to a bender. Even though it will eventually come back, it will render them useless in more than one way as they lose control of their limbs as well as all possibility to bend themselves away.

It may seem weird that you will learn from this, seeing that it is meant to block people like you from bending. Knowing about it will help you lookout for it. There will always be people out there who are looking for ways to knock you off your game. For instance, if you are trying to lose weight, someone with ill intent may say discouraging things to you on how they haven't noticed a difference or whatnot. This could temporarily discourage you from wanting to pursue your goal for the time being. But it doesn't mean you can't jump back in.

Instead, you need to learn to do your own chi blocking to counter these people. Instead of them temporarily discouraging you, you need to discourage them from attempting to attack you maliciously. Think of it as Ty Lee chi blocking Azula to protect her friend, Mai, from being fried to a crisp in the episode *The Boiling Rock part 2*. As you see a person going for the tender points, dodge and go for something that will shut it down. How this would work is like so, a person mentions how you still look fat even though you mentioned you lost a few pounds. It can be heartbreaking to hear this, but instead of taking it and falling off the path, you're responding in a way to dismiss it. You could respond with "It's a start and I'm starting to feel better and not as sluggish as before." Comebacks with positive reinforcement to what you are doing, not acknowledging the hurtful comments and something beyond that they were commenting on will stop them in their tracks. Each time they try to throw a shot at you, bring your positive energy and outlook of your journey and shoot it back at them.

In a way, you will be blocking the part of them that wants to criticize you and the part of them that's negative. They will be thrown off and forced to look at something positive. Enough times and they may start falling for the idea of looking at life like you do. Not that chi blocking really does that, it's only temporary. Though you can never tell what might come out of telling people the positive aspects of your journey.

This of course can also be used to help others. If you see someone picking on someone, and it's obviously not a funny joke to the victim, step in and block the oppressor. There is no need to get physical to do it this way either. Use more words of reinforcement to help the victim. Maybe even try explaining why what is happening is wrong. Read the situation and strike with your best judgment. It isn't as clear as a map of chi points to follow, though you'll over time find them and memorize them like they are your ABC's.

<u>Creativity</u>

Varrick is one of the only non-benders that isn't trained to fight. We see him try in mech suits at one point, though his strengths are clearly in creating. We see him range in escape plans, organized crime, movers, inventions, and even beams made from spirit vine energy. The man is everywhere with everything! Not to mention the creative thinking Zhu Li has to do when all he says is "Zhu Li do the thing!" It's like she needs to read his mind, or has to become his mind as maybe he might not truly know what he needs at the moment.

Creativity is a skill we all have in some form or another. Varrick though makes it who he is. There is creative bending from Aang creating the air scooter and Katara getting water from her own sweat, but nothing has been as impactful as Varrick's ideas. Varrick's entire idea of the Nuttuck movers was to persuade people to support the South Pole in the civil war. His discovery of what spirit vine energy can do led to catastrophic damage to republic city, ultimately creating a brand new spirit portal. Those were only two instances, not to mention the crimes he pulled off and sometimes escaped from.

The lesson here is how you become as creative as Varrick. There are a few ways that you can go about this. There are daily practices you can do to boost your creativity and there are extreme ways to get creative ideas. Varrick is more of the latter, though you don't have to do that to get the results you are looking for. Dabble in these tricks to boost creativity, there is something out there for everyone.

The basics of boosting creativity are similar to what you already have learned. Creativity just didn't come up as it wasn't the focus for the exercise in the elements. The idea is a clear head to help the creative ideas flow. If your mind is cluttered, there are chances that you won't see those ideas you've been counting on. Kind of like how you can't focus on relaxing on the couch if there is a huge pile of dishes in the kitchen. Make sure to practice meditation as well as make sure your environment is clutter-free wherever you are when needing an idea. The concept of going for a walk to clear your head can come into play here. If you can reach the daydreamy state that was talked about for mala bead meditation, then you will find that ideas will show themselves more easily. This is why ideas come up a lot when driving, going to bed, or in the shower.

Daily activities are doing physical creative activities. Consider drawing, writing, playing an instrument, crafting anything that will involve some level of creative thinking. It doesn't have to be strenuous, just something you can let yourself get lost at doing for a little bit each day. This is essentially practice for the mind to be creative. Keep using it and it will start to grow and before you know it, you'll be ten times more creative than you were when you started.

Now for the Varrick method. Varrick strives to stay at the forefront of imagination, innovation, or in his words "Imagination." By doing this he undergoes a process of intense practices to increase blood circulation. His method does have truth behind it. Increased blood flow to the brain will give it more oxygen and help it perform better. The part that doesn't need to happen to achieve this necessarily is eating hot peppers and hanging upside down. There are other ways to increase blood flow than a whole shebang that will ultimately hurt your stomach. Exercise is a great way to increase blood flow. When you exercise, blood flow increases all throughout the body. While running and heavy lifting can accomplish this, walking can also raise the blood flow a little bit. This is why it's recommended to get up and walk around after sitting for long periods of time. It's healthy for the body but the increased blood flow will also help your performance on whatever you are working on.

Recalling from earlier, laughter meditation can also improve your creativity. See it as a stress reliever that will give your mind more room to think. Anything that helps you relax can be used to help clear the mind and create more ideas. If this is longing outside listening to the world around you, then do that to help invite your ideas in. Varrick isn't much of a relaxer, but that doesn't mean you can't!

<u>Equality</u>

While it's important to not pick up bad habits from villains, you can learn from them. In this case, look at all the non-benders involved in the equalist movement. They strove for equality, fearing the oppression of benders. This fight for equality started long ago as non-benders made machines for factories so that they could work in them and not have to rely on benders. This didn't mean factories with benders didn't exist. This felt threatening to many benders where they had a feud going on between the two. When Aang visited a business council meeting in the comic *Imbalance.* The feud was so prominent that benders would sit on one side as non-benders would sit on the other side.

It can be obvious that everything should be equal to all people in the series. But at what part is it going too far? Hiroshi Sato was grief-stricken by the loss of his wife to a fire bender, so much so he felt the only way to correct one bender's wrongdoings was to destroy all benders. This is where the lesson is. It is possible to be too extreme in a belief to where it will harm others.

When one person does something wrong, it should not inflict an entire group to not exist. Unless the entire group is at fault for wrongdoing, there is no justice by punishing all the innocent members of a group or community. Think back to grade school. If a kid was doing something bad, they were individually punished. Though, there were times when only some kids were doing something bad and the entire class got in trouble. How did you feel about that then if you were one of the innocent bystanders? Now, what if the whole class participates in doing something bad and everyone gets punished? It seems fairer than the middle scenario. Think of life like this. If you see one person who is part of a group do something wrong, why would you pin it on the whole group? But if a whole group participates then it seems reasonable to expect them all to face justice.

Things won't always be black and white in life. The grey areas in life will take time to evaluate, but it can be easy to jump to conclusions of an entire group of people. Suddenly you think you know all of them due to one person's or a few people's actions. Where is the equality in that? The equalists had reasons to point blame at all benders, though was it fair when Hiroshi blamed Mako and Korra for his wife's death when they weren't the benders involved? Take this scenario with you as you fight for equality.

Equality is something that should also not be ignored. There are people in this world that suffer more than others, struggle in day-to-day life from things the majority may not even think about. This is where you can step in and fight for the victims of inequality. There is much to learn from them. Emptying your cup will be essential when learning of the struggles of victims. Take what you learn to help better the world for them. Use your Avatar training to fight the rest of the way. Keep in mind those affected when you fight for equality to not create a new inequality.

<u>Bringing It All Together</u>

All of these skills have been noted to where they relate back to your training. The key is to integrate them into your daily life and practices so that you may become more well-rounded in how the world works and to be able to help others. As a bender, these are things that wouldn't have come to you as easy as they do to a non-bender. As they see the world differently, knowing the backbone of these people will help you create a better world overall.

There is a possibility of mixing these skills and lessons together on their own as well. Think of how strategic planning can go with helping true equality thrive in the world. Resourceful and strategic planning also work very well together if you focus on them. Part of the fun is trying different things with what you've learned from your non-bender friends. Possibilities are endless, another lesson you could say comes from them. There will always be a way to bring someone up to another's level. The determination and intelligence of a non-bender cannot be competed with, it is what they drive on.

Do not take these lessons as the only things you'll ever need to learn and know about, there is always more to learn. These, in the end, are some of the stand-out traits. Like all humans, they are also very complex. And with the amount of variety you get, you can learn so many different things about the world around you. Never ignore a chance to learn more and to return the opportunity by helping when you can.

How You Will Know You Are Ready

Like before when you evaluated yourself after learning the four elements, you will be scoring yourself to see your mastery of non-bending. As before, here is a checklist to measure where you are. Each item should be scored on a 1-10 rating. 1 is the lowest indicating that you have nothing and have only read the section. 10 will be the highest and means you are confident in the work you have done in that section and see no more need to improve it. Add up the scores at the end and look at your overall score. Think of it as a letter grade in school, 90-100 is an A, 80-89 is a B, 70-79 is a C, 60-69 is a D and everything below that is an F. The goal here is to reach for an A. While other scores are considered passing, they don't indicate mastery. You could move on in the average level grades such as B and C, but be aware that your non-bending skills will only be as good as you practice them.

___ You have grown to own your own personal power.

___ You are aware and put effort into being everyone's Avatar.

___ You have implemented being resourceful into your life.

___ You take time in all situations to stop and strategically plan.

___ You are able to hide your fear in situations you need to show your brave face.

___ You have mastered not taking everything so seriously.

___ You have mastered and used Chi Blocking when it is called for.
___You have implemented daily practices to increase your creativity.
___ You understand how to avoid extreme equality.

___ You understand and have mastered all the non-bending skills.

____ Overall Score

Avatar State

<u>What The Avatar State Means to Us</u>

The Avatar State is a spiritual experience where you will be able to reach the untapped potential that lies within you. In the series, we see the act of the Avatar State awaken a blue light within the Avatar's eyes, giving them the power of all the Avatars before them. Unleashing this abundance of power doesn't just happen, though. To achieve this power, you will be training like Aang did with Guru Pathik in the episode *The Guru*, by using chakra theory and meditation. This practice is not associated with a single faith or religion, as it can be used to enlighten and understand yourself more while participating in your own spiritual beliefs.

Before attempting to open the chakras, you must understand why they must be opened. Up until now in your everyday life, you have only been able to use up to 10-15% of your brain. This includes physical sensation, emotions, and thoughts. The chakras are a network of energy that locate up the spine to the top of the head, directly into the brain. These seven chakras all connect to the brain as they influence your physical, emotions, and thinking. To open and use properly will lead you to more mastery over yourself.

Each chakra is a center of influence for particular emotions and thoughts as you will learn. As you go through your training, you will notice which ones are most prominent in your life. You will also see more clearly who you are, or your samskara. Samskaras are the mental impressions that we have on ourselves of who we are. Not what we can see in a mirror, but who we are once we take the body away. The samskara is what influences our karmas, or in other words our tendencies in the world. Think of it as the good and bad energy discussed in the fire element. What we do directly affects the world around us, with that in mind, it is extremely important to understand ourselves so we may do what is right.

Within the chakras are three bodies. The first one is the physical, which is the location where they are. The second one is astral. The astral body of the chakra is the emotion that the particular chakra influences. Many times it will be a bilinear spectrum with opposite emotions on each side. From there you will learn to understand the emotions and create balance within them. The third body is the causal. The causal is the dimension of thought. Thoughts may create emotions and emotions may create thoughts, though they are separate entities.

Understanding the separations of these bodies will help understand yourself as you discover your own samskara. Taking yourself out of your body and looking down at who you are will lead you to the ultimate realization of your influence on the world around you. Guru Pathik described the system to Aang as something similar to a stream with different pools it flows through. If one gets clogged by debris, the water cannot flow down the stream. If you find and remove the clog, the water flows effortlessly. This is why you must approach the chakras from an outside view looking within. There you will see what debris is disrupting the flow of your chakra. The parts of you that you don't realize are bringing negative energy into the world could be your downfall. Find them, acknowledge that part of yourself, and work toward a better version of yourself.

Contacting Your Past Lives

Before you begin the chakra training, try contacting your past lives. They are the backbone of your Avatar State as you summon all their powers when using it. The most powerful thing they can give you is knowledge from their own experiences. By contacting your past lives, you will be surrounded by a multitude of options as you face your own challenges.

Reaching your past lives won't actually summon ghosts to come to talk to you. This is a visualization practice that you can do to put yourself into others' shoes. The visualization of a conversation with your past lives will help make the options more real. When you just think about what someone would do in a situation, you can be biased as you let your own prejudices take over. When you are in a conversation with a person, you will get what they mean wholeheartedly. Think of Zuko when he was doing an impression of Azula when brainstorming what she would do to join the Avatar's team. He exaggerated his movements and his words. It was mocking what the person would do in a theatrical way. When we see Azula confront people to do something, it's more methodical and true to how she would handle a situation. Take the person out of your mind and face them in conversation.

Reaching them comes from meditation. Clear your head, close your eyes, and focus on the empty space in front of you. Visualize into existence the form of a past life. You could go multiple different routes on what you consider a past life. One way is to picture your own ancestors. Fill in the gaps of what you don't know about them based on the information you already do know. Secondly, you could call on historical figures that you look up to such as Gandhi, Martin Luther King Jr., or Abraham Lincoln. If you look up to them, chances are you have a feeling of how they think. You will be surprised by what they tell you from their life that can help yours. Lastly, you can contact the Avatars from the series. Start with one and go down the line of Avatars until you are satisfied.

Your past lives will each individually bring something new to the table as all people face different challenges in their lives. Different backgrounds. If you wanted to mix the three categories up, you could. Make your line up with your great-grandma, William Shakespeare, and Avatar Aang if that feels right for you. You can have several past lives you regularly contact. A pool of different kinds of people will give you more perspectives than a perspective of a single group. That's why the Avatar is able to contact more than the most previous past life, to reach the different perspectives of different nations.

The conversation doesn't have to be a long one. Long enough for them to tell you how they see things, how they handled a similar situation, and how they believe in you. A friendly relationship between you and your past lives will strengthen the connection. It won't just be an image of someone, but it will feel like a part of you. Don't be afraid to let the conversation be heartfelt or humorous at times. Human interactions aren't always serious, and your interactions with your past lives shouldn't be any different.

<u>Earth Chakra</u>

The first Chakra to be looked at is the Earth Chakra, also known as the Root, Base, or Muladhara chakra. This chakra's physical location is at the bottom of the spine, within the gonads. Imagine it as a flower, where the base of it starts at your back and points forward. The front is where the chakra will open and allow its energy to flow out and up the chakra system. To evaluate how this chakra is doing, look for its physical symptoms such as sexual health and urinary health. When the karmas and samskaras are bad, there you may find dysfunction and infection.

The most adequate way to describe this chakra in the astral embodiment would be anger. Anger should not be taken as a negative emotion here, as it has a spectrum of its own. The good anger that you should strive for is the anger that enacts change. Think of it as a seed that's been planted in the ground. It must use its anger for change to break out of the soil and grow. If you feel anger for how something is in the world, use that emotion to create change. This is where you will see anger in its purest form when it is used selflessly to change things for the better.

Anger will be bad and destructive if it becomes egotistical. If it's geared towards your personal likes and dislikes it will become destructive. Imagine a kid who wants a cookie but is denied one. In anger, they will throw a fit, throw insults and break things. It's crucial you evaluate your anger to recognize it before this happens. While it's nice to want things, many people can become hurt if you let yourself stop at nothing to get it.

Guru Pathik described this chakra to Aang as survival that can be blocked by fears and anxieties. Think of it as survival, if you don't grow you will never reach the ultimate goal. When you let yourself be bogged down by fear you start to be rash. Anxieties tend to stop people in their tracks as if they are deer in the headlights. Survival isn't getting the cookie, but having proper nutrition. Sure the cookie would be a delicious treat, but it's not worth tearing others down to get it when there are other options to help yourself and help the world.

In the causal thought, you think about bodily existence. You will ask where you are physically, astrally (emotionally), and causally (thinking). You are able to pinpoint where you are in these categories. Physically you are here reading this book. Physically you are at the base of the spine where the chakra resides. You can ask yourself where you are astrally. You can ask where your causal self is. There is no wrong way to ask this question, but your answers can help understand where you are astrally. Where are you emotionally with where you are right now?

Practicing meditation for the chakras can be intense, but for beginners, start with the basic. Here will be basic meditation for the chakra. Once you are ready to dive into chakra meditation more, there will be resources at the end of this book for you. For now, let's focus on a meditation practice for just the earth chakra.

Start by going to your meditation stance. From there, you will have to breathe into the diaphragm but not the chest. Once the belly extends outwards, make sure to keep the glottis in the throat open. To do this, keep the pressure on the stomach, do not relax. If you relax you will feel the air go up but be stuck trying to get past the throat. From the position of having a deep breath in the stomach and the glottis open, concentrate on the area where this chakra resides. Now, constrict inwardly the anus and genital areas tightly. Once you feel the urge to breathe out, relax the area and slowly release the breathe. Repeat this several times. In the event, you need to catch your breath between repetitions, do so. This is a chakra meditation, not a breathing exercise. If you feel strange energy where the chakra is, that is normal. That is the chakra opening.

<table>
<tr><td colspan="2">Earth Chakra quick facts</td></tr>
<tr><td>Color</td><td>Red</td></tr>
<tr><td>Stones</td><td>Emerald
Carnelian</td></tr>
<tr><td>Deities</td><td>Brahma
Dakini</td></tr>
<tr><td>Aromatherapy</td><td>Cedarwood
Patchouli
Myrrh</td></tr>
<tr><td>Other areas it deals with</td><td>Sexuality
Stability
Sensuality
Security</td></tr>
</table>

Water Chakra

The next chakra is the water chakra, also known as the sacral or Svadhishthana chakra. Physically, it shares the same function as the earth chakra. Problems with genitals, the bladder, or kidneys could also be linked to this chakra. Though you will find its position on the spine to be higher than the earth chakra. Between the groin and the navel is where you will find this chakra. Again, imagine a flower with the base pointed at the back and the opening at the front.

The astral emotions of this chakra are fear and lust. Think of these opposites as "I desperately want that" and "I'm desperately afraid of that." Both are very primitive in nature as you crave for pleasures hungrily, sexually, and for survival. You become fearful as these pleasures are taken from you. If someone is going to snatch food from your plate without consent, you will strike their hand or call them out on it. These emotions are essential for survival, though leaning too much into either of them can cause an imbalance.

These emotions can be a lot to handle when opening this chakra. Samskaras of sexuality and physicality arise from this. When this chakra starts to open for the first time in a person, it is when a person starts transition into a teenager. They become moody. They don't have the handle on the intense emotions of fear and lust. Everything seems like the end of the world to them. They become easily attracted to peers around them. They may lash out at a simple question. They do not know how to navigate through these emotions, yet it is thrown at them with full force. Even adults find they struggle with these emotions. One thing is out of place and you lash out at your spouse, coworker, or friend.

Guru Pathik discussed fear with Aang during his training. Fear in the form of guilt. Aang was plagued with the fear of being separated from his beloved teacher but now felt guilty. His fear rose to what he had done, not allowing himself to feel at peace with what had happened. By fearing his guilt, he wasn't open to receiving any form of pleasure. On a scale, he was too far along on the fear side. Look for the inner balance of the scale.

In the causal thought, you will find yourself creating justifications. These justifications are a mask created to hide your primitive impulses. Imagine someone is talking to you and says something that irritates you. You immediately tell them to shut up and lash out. Later when you think about it, you may conclude you were hungry or that they should have known not to say that to you. In reality, you had an impulse to quiet the person, though nothing else made you do it.

Think of it as justifying your desires. Such as "I deserve to have pizza for dinner because I had a bad day." The craving for pizza wasn't made by the bad day. The bad day helped your mind justify its want for pizza. Notice when these things happen. It becomes a habit to try and hide our instinctual impulses. Fearing the embarrassment you may face. Having people see you in a way you do not care for. To overcome this, you must become honest with yourself. Being honest with why you want something or did something will help you to see your true self. To see the samskaras and karmas for what they really are. Denying this will only lead you down a path of unresolved issues.

To work with this chakra in meditation you will begin in your meditative stance. From there you will breathe into the diaphragm and keep the glottis open. Once you do that, bring in the lower abdomen. Hold that tension until you feel the breath naturally wanting to be let go. Release all tension as you breathe out. Repeat this several times with breathing breaks as needed.

Water Chakra Quick Facts	
Color	Orange
Stones	Fire Opal
	Carnelian
Deities	Vishnu
	Rakini
Aromatherapy	Sandalwood
	Jasmine
	Rose
Other areas it deals with	Reproduction
	Creativity
	Joy
	Enthusiasm

Fire Chakra

The third chakra is the fire chakra, also known as the solar plexus or manipura chakra. Physically, this chakra is found in the digestive system. Between the navel and the sternum, you will find it along the spine behind the solar plexus. Sensing something is wrong with this chakra is found in your digestion. Everyone has stomach issues from time to time, though that isn't necessarily an indicator for chakra problems. If the issues are habitual, then there is room to be concerned about it.

When you look at the astral emotions within this chakra, you will find worry and contentment. Think of it as butterflies in your stomach when you get nervous about a presentation. If you are constantly worried, you may find that your stomach aches more, food doesn't settle. You may even find that worrying brings on binge eating. Many people with issues with the fire chakra tend to have weight problems. That is from the relationship the astral and physical body has together in this chakra.

Contentment is found when you aren't tied up in worry. Things seem to go your way. You tend to live in the present and focus on that. When you throw the future into the mix, this is where you start to stir up the chakra. Suddenly you don't crave all the fatty foods when you already ate. Your stomach doesn't gargle at you after eating. This is what it means to be content.

The causal thoughts of this chakra can be a huge influencer on the emotions you experience. It deals with thoughts of fearing the future. It can be easy to be swept up in the grand scheme of things. Wondering what will happen if something doesn't work out or if you lose your job and all of the things that could happen to you. Even on this journey as you look at your secret tunnel, looking at everything you have to accomplish. This is why you should focus on one step at a time. Looking at anything in the future can only give you worry and stress.

Guru Pathik talks to Aang about willpower when they reach this chakra. Aang's shame for accidentally burning Katara stops him from wanting to learn how to fire bend. The worry within his mind stops him from reaching his true potential. You must realize this with the shame you carry within yourself. What is in the past is in the past. You can do better now that you have learned, though you need to carry on and try.

In your chakra meditation, resume your meditative stance. From there, you will breathe into the diaphragm and keep the glottis open. Now, bring in the upper adamant and hold it. Once you reach the limit and your breathe wants to be released, slowly let it out and relax the upper abdomen. Repeat several times with breathing breaks as needed.

Fire Chakra Quick Facts

Color	Yellow
Stones	Topaz
	Yellow Tourmaline
	Sapphire
Deities	Rudra
	Lakini
Aromatherapy	Clary Sage
	Juniper
	Geranium
Other areas it deals with	Digestion
	Power
	Expansiveness
	Growth

Uncle Iroh's Wisdom

"Pride is not the opposite of shame but its source. True humility is the only antidote to shame."

When we feel shame, we are often trying to protect ourselves with our pride. We fear letting people see us down and in a bad light. To cure this, become humble. Admit what happened and look forward to striving to be better than before. Letting it go will be the only way to get rid of it.

The fourth chakra is the Heart chakra, also known as anahata. The location on the spine for this one can be found by squeezing the shoulders back against each other. The opening goes out towards your front, behind the sternum. The organ this chakra is in is the circulatory system. Your heart, as it sends blood throughout the body, also sends out the energy of the chakras to help the body. When you face habitual heart complications, this is when you will look into the anahata with concern.

Looking into the astral emotions of this chakra, you will deal with joy and jealousy. Joy could be about numerous things such as accomplishments with the self or good fortune for others. This is what we ultimately thrive for. Watching those you care about succeeding and feeling true joy for them leaves a warm sensation within.

Jealousy can easily consume a person. You ask why so and so got something but not you. There is a burning emotion you feel where you believe you should have fortune over others, yet reality says something different. There is no eliminating jealousy as it is instinctual. Even animals are controlled by jealousy. If you pet one dog in front of the other, chances are the dog will get jealous and will butt in or whine. Humans are no different. It starts becoming problematic when it becomes egotistical. When you get on your high horse and truly believe you deserve everything others are getting, that you are better than them. This is where you need to look inside yourself and humble yourself. Look for joy instead of jealousy.

The causal thought is where you have judgmental thoughts such as right and wrong. It's when a person looks at a person of a different religion than them and says "that's just not right." They give a justification of why it isn't right. What they believe is the only right thing in their eyes. A sense of right and wrong isn't necessarily a bad thing. It's these thoughts that help us to help others. This becomes a bad thing when you let your ego control it. You feel more righteous than others because of your political and religious beliefs. The feeling that the world would be a better place without Joe blow because they didn't vote for your political party. These thoughts are driven by your own ego to make you seem better than those around you. Be aware of your thoughts and correct them when they overstep a boundary. There is a difference between saying something is wrong because you have a different religious view and going to help someone being attacked. One is influenced by your own self-interest and the other is driven by the morals of someone else's safety.

Meditation for this chakra will be slightly different than the previous three. Still, resume your meditative stance. When you breathe in, fill up and extend the chest. The glottis will be half-open as you inhale and exhale. To do this, you hear a grunting sound as you breathe in and out. It will feel throaty as you do it. Concentrating on the chest, you will breathe in with the glottis half-open, hold and then release the breath as you relax the chest and keep the glottis half-open. Repeat this several times with breathing breaks as needed.

Heart Chakra Quick Facts

Color	Green (also pink, red, or white)
Stones	Peridot
	Pink Topaz
	Rhodonite
	Rose Quartz
Deities	Ishvara
	Kakini
Aromatherapy	Rose
	Melissa
	Neroli
Other areas it deals with	Unconditional Love
	Love
	Circulation
	Passion
	Devotion

<u>Sound Chakra</u>

The fifth chakra is the sounds chakra, also known as the throat and vishuddha chakra. On the spine you can find it on the base of the curve to the neck, opening forward through the throat. Physically it is the respiratory system. Think of the breath and how it reacts to the body's status. When the body burns more energy you breathe more. It carries its energy through the air you breathe. When habitual problems arise in these areas, look at this chakra.

Astral emotions with this chakra will target your attachment, producing grief and poignancy. Grieving for what is lost is a natural thing. Taking the time to grieve can be a very beneficial thing. Poignancy, the act of accepting something that has happened, is what is strived for. This does not mean you prefer the loss that happened, but you still accept it and no longer carry regret.

There is a story of apprentices approaching their master and asking about non-attachment. The master shows them a beautiful glass he received as a gift. He told them that it is beautiful, but it is already broken in his mind. It's about acceptance that all things will either break or living beings will die. If you see what is in your life like this, there will be no fear of when something unfortunate happens. You will have accepted that it is a part of life. But remember that between now and then, their presence is a beautiful thing. Enjoy what is around you now as you have it instead of worrying about preserving it.

The causal thought in this chakra is your control of attention and reflection. When you are not able to keep your attention, your sound chakra is weak. Attention doesn't necessarily mean just listening to others, it also has to do with your own speech. If you are telling a story and keep making side comments that lead you down a rabbit hole where you have to think of where you left off in the story, your attention is weak. Pay attention to the point you are making.

Guru Pathik conversed with Aang more on the reflection side of this chakra. He talks about the truth. In reflection, you look back to what has happened. In many cases, it's like a game of telephone, where you say one thing in a person's ear and they go down the line and you see what the person at the end heard. Many times the words get twisted around. The goal is to not have distortion when remembering the past. The distortion you create will create lies to help you feel better. Practice paying attention and you will find your reflection will improve.

In the meditation for this chakra, resume your meditative position. Take in a normal deep breath and close the glottis by relaxing the belly and chest. You will feel the pressure at the bottom of your throat, which is the glottis holding it in. Hold this breath until it starts to strain, then let it out. Repeat several times with breathing brakes as needed.

<table>
<tr><td colspan="2">Sound Chakra Quick Facts</td></tr>
<tr><td>Color</td><td>Turquoise</td></tr>
<tr><td>Stones</td><td>Blue Topaz</td></tr>
<tr><td></td><td>Yellow Topaz</td></tr>
<tr><td></td><td>Quartz</td></tr>
<tr><td>Deities</td><td>Sadasiva</td></tr>
<tr><td></td><td>Sakini</td></tr>
<tr><td>Aromatherapy</td><td>Lavender</td></tr>
<tr><td></td><td>Chamomile</td></tr>
<tr><td></td><td>Rosemary</td></tr>
<tr><td></td><td>Thyme</td></tr>
<tr><td></td><td>Sage</td></tr>
<tr><td>Other areas it deals with</td><td>Expression</td></tr>
<tr><td></td><td>Communication</td></tr>
<tr><td></td><td>Fluent Thought</td></tr>
<tr><td></td><td>Independence</td></tr>
<tr><td></td><td>Security</td></tr>
</table>

<u>Light Chakra</u>

The sixth chakra is the Light chakra, also known as the brow, third eye, or ajna chakra. The base of this chakra is found at the base of the skull where the spine enters it. The opening of the chakra faces forward between the brow lines. In some artwork, you may find it depicted as a third eye in the middle of the forehead. This chakra controls the central nervous system of the body. Habitual problems with this system can indicate problems with this chakra.

The Astral emotion of this chakra is transcendent bliss. Think of this as being happy even though nothing works out the way you wanted. It can be hard to imagine feeling that way as you go through all your daily anxieties. Getting to this state isn't as complicated as you think though. At a point, you start to feel overwhelmed, calm yourself. Use yoga, meditation, a walk, or anything that brings you to a stay of calm. The emotion will start to kick in when you enter the phase where nothing can touch you because you are in such a pleasurable state.

The causal thoughts will be your reasoning without the influence of prejudices. You are seeing the world without your own beliefs and opinions to entertain how others see things. This will help you strengthen your own beliefs and faiths. For example, let's say you are a Christian. If a person comes up to you and says they don't believe in God, do not take it as an offense. Ask why they believe that. Entertain what they have to say without adding in any of your own beliefs. If you take the person's stance and put it up against your own afterward, you have two choices. One is to adopt the new belief because you see it as better than your own. The second one is to reject the stance, allowing you to strengthen your own faith. Taking in new stances will give you the opportunity to examine your own faith and solidify it as you point out your own reasons for practicing it.

Aang is taught about the illusion of separation when he opens this chakra. Removing this prejudiced form of thinking will allow you to see people as their basic self, rather than seeing all the things you may agree or disagree with. In the end, we all are born with a clean slate. We learn what to think and how to act. When you remove that, your reasoning goes to a basic idea of human existence. While we have borders, political parties, faiths, social classes, gender, sexes, race, and many other categories, we are still all connected as a human race. Removing the labels when we see the world will give our own mind a constant, where other factors cannot determine our own opinions.

To meditate on this chakra, resume your meditative stance. When you breathe in, imagine the energy rising from the root chakra up to the light chakra base. From there, keep the glottis open and slowly nod your head forward. You should feel an energy presence on the top of your head that moves downward on the forehead as you nod downward. Once it's over the lower forehead, stop moving the head. When you are ready to release the breath, gently nod your head upwards and release the breath. Repeat this several times with breathing breaks as needed.

Light Chakra Quick Facts

Color	Deep Blue or white
Stones	Diamonds
	Emerald
	Sapphire
Deities	Shiva
	Shakti hakini
Aromatherapy	Frankincense
	Basil
Other areas it deals with	Intuition
	Clarity
	Meditation

<u>Thought Chakra</u>

The last chakra is the thought chakra, also known as the crown or Sahasrara chakra. This chakra sits at the top of the system, on the crown of the head. Here it is also connected to the central nervous system. This chakra is different from the others as it is not a flower releasing energy. This one is like a gateway you will learn. First, you must understand the other embodiments it has.

The astral emotion is transcendent bliss, just like the light chakra. It is a different bliss, though. This one is reached without having to enter a trance. Instead, this one happens naturally after lots of practice with the chakras. Suddenly you will eat, sleep and live life in the bliss that no worry can touch you. You will not obsess over the daily struggles that you face. You will feel at peace in daily life.

The causal thought is consciousness. This is not being awake and seeing the world around you, it goes deeper than that. This is you seeing yourself without the body. The gateway of the chakra is to take you out of the body and see yourself without the labels put on you. There is no gender, race, ethnicity, age, or any label set upon a human when you look at yourself without the body. When Guru Pathik told Aang to let go once he reached this chakra, he was asking him to look at himself without his body. To see who he really is from the astral realm. To realize he exists beyond his own body.

Practicing this in meditation will bring you to the consciousness of who you are. There is much that can be said of who you are here in this book that is something you need to see for yourself. From there, you can see who you are and what you need to work on. What you need to improve on.

To meditate with this chakra, resume your normal meditative stance. Put your tongue on the roof of your mouth. This will create a passageway for the energy you are about to meditate on. There is no breathing exercise to go with this one, it is primarily visual. Imagine the energy in the top of your head going down the front of your face through the chakras. It will travel from the roof of the mouth to the tongue and to the throat in this journey. Once it reaches the sound chakra in the throat, imagine it dispersing all throughout the body as if it is the roots of a tree reaching out to all parts of the soil. Keep imagining it for as long as you need. You may even gently tilt the head back if it helps the visualization for you.

Thought Chakra Quick Facts	
Color	Violet
Stones	Celestite
	Blue Sapphire
	Charoite
Deities	Shiva
	Shakti
Aromatherapy	Ylang-ylang
	Rosewood
	Linden
	Lotus
Other areas it deals with	Release of Karma
	Universal Consciousness
	Beigness
	Unity

<u>Using the Avatar State</u>

Using the Avatar State is a gift. After working with your chakras, you can use your new found power to positively influence the world. There is no guideline for how or when you must use this state. What you must keep in mind though, is that you must continue to revisit the chakras to keep them open. You are only able to reach your full potential when they are functioning correctly. If you notice jealousy coming more easily to you, focus time on the heart chakra. Jealousy could bring your ego into your decisions and taint them with bias.

Having spiritual enlightenment and clarity can open many doors for you. If you are not focused on materialistic, egotistical, or moral conquest, you will see the world will come to you easier. It's like the example from before, a parent should put their air mask on before putting it on the child. You need to know and be aware of yourself so if things start to crumble, you know that won't be one of the things. Continue to strengthen your connections to the chakras.

It is almost impossible to use the Avatar State for personal gain, as so many have you letting go of emotions and attachments. To fully enter it, you are surrendering yourself to help those around you. Money and other attachments won't be the driving force anymore but helping them will be. It's not to say you can't want to work for those things, they just won't be priority number one when you use the Avatar State.

If you are contemplating if you should use it for something, then go through entering it. If you are fully immersed in your Avatar State and still feel and see the need to do something, then it will be the time to use it. But if you go into this mindset and feel that you would be doing something for personal gain and that's all, you will know that it is not the time to use your new found power. It can be handy to go into it, having your full mind and body focused on your legacy with no outside factors. This can be what helps guide you to success as the Avatar.

<u>There Will Always Be Vaatu</u>

Finally, when understanding the Avatar State, you must realize it is more than just your past lives that are with you. The Great Spirit, Raava is also within you. This spirit brings goodness and light within you. Your drive to do good in the world and help others succeed. Raava is there to help you as well as there to let you spread her light on the world.

This also means that Raava's other half, Vaatu, the great spirit of darkness also exists. He does not reside within you, though he will try and pursue you. The world seems grim at times. The media blasts the unfortunate news like it's going out of style. Our minds are so fixated on it that we forget the goodness humanity has. Just as the great spirits battle on harmonic convergence, you must also take a battle against darkness. Become the light within others as you strive to see and create more light.

What you need to understand the most about the darkness is that it will never totally disappear. Just like light, it will always exist. There will never be a day where a tragedy doesn't happen in the world. That also means that there isn't a single day that goes by where there aren't good, righteous deeds happening. Highlight those events in your mind, focus on them. Darkness will never be vanquished but it can be subdued and kept that way.

What you can do in your lifetime is to help light shine brightly. To help people find their own light. Every day is a new opportunity to make a difference. Do as much as you can, but don't be discouraged when you still see darkness in the world. Your job isn't to eliminate it, but to show people a better alternative to it.

Uncle Iroh's Wisdom
"If you look for the light, you will often find it. But if you look for the dark, that is all you will ever see."

Iroh speaks these words to Korra as she feels small and hopeless. She focused on what she could not do instead of what she could do. This would bring negatively tainted spirits around her. But once she started looking for the light, she was able to overcome those fears and was able to help the poor injured spirit back home. This rings true in our own lives as if we only focus on what's wrong with the world, we often see all the good things that happen around us. There is no hope of happiness if you only keep your eye on the darkness. Instead, even in bad times, look for the light and you will find it fighting within all the darkness that rests in the world.

How You Will Know You Are Ready

Like before when you evaluated yourself after learning the four elements and non-bending, you will be scoring yourself to see your mastery of the Avatar State. As before, here is a checklist to measure where you are. Each item should be scored on a 1-10 rating. 1 is the lowest indicating that you have nothing and have only read the section. 10 will be the highest and means you are confident in the work you have done in that section and see no more need to improve it. Add up the scores at the end and look at your overall score. Think of it as a letter grade in school, 90-100 is an A, 80-89 is a B, 70-79 is a C, 60-69 is a D and everything below that is an F. The goal here is to reach for an A. While other scores are considered passing, they don't indicate mastery. You could move on in the average level grades such as B and C, but be aware that the Avatar State will only work if you fully accomplish the training.

___ You are able to contact your past lives using visualization.

___ You have opened the Earth Chakra.

216

___ You have opened the Water Chakra.

___ You have opened the Fire Chakra.

___ You have opened the Heart Chakra.

___ You have opened the Sound Chakra.

___ You have opened the Light chakra.

___ You have opened the Thought Chakra.

___ You are fully aware of when and how to use the Avatar State.

___ You are fully aware that there will always be darkness, though you can overcome it.

____ Overall Score

Conclusion

<u>You Are a Full-Fledged Avatar</u>

No longer a half-baked Avatar, you are ready to live up to your Avatar destiny. As a full-fledged Avatar, you are now ready to better the world and reach the life you have always dreamed of. Over the course of this guide, you have mastered Earth, Fire, Air, and Water. You have learned important skills from non-benders. Gained your own Team Avatar. You have even mastered the Avatar State. Now, you have all the power you need to do anything.

It may be a bittersweet feeling to get to this point. After dedicating yourself for so long to training and mastering your Avatarhood, you are now free to do as you please. Enjoy the fruits of your labor. With what you have built, there will be no worrying if life comes to try and take you down. You have the tools to stand strong and perceiver. Looking back, see how much your foundation has grown and holds you up as you go through life. See how your energy and willpower burn within you and are used to their fullest extent. See how free you are as if you were wind. See how skilled you are in aiding people with healing. The four elements now live within you and are in your control, no longer will you be controlled by outside forces.

Compare where your knowledge of the world was at the beginning and now. See how much you've learned about different people. Look at the understanding you have created within yourself. The love you have for all who walk on this Earth. You are here to serve all and to make this world a marvelous place to live. No biased opinions will sway you from the truth. Nothing will stand in your way for defending the truth. You are fully capable of using your knowledge for good and to balance the world.

Think back to what you knew about yourself before you started this journey. How little you truly understood why you were the way you were. Not enough discipline to control the elements yet. Trying to strive for something without acknowledging the true reasons you weren't there yet. Now, you are aware of yourself and why you do and feel things. You are able to control yourself in stressful situations and help your inner wounds. You no longer let anything hold you back. You are in complete control of yourself.

Take a moment to see how much easier you are able to help others with the control of your chakras, your Avatar State. How you are able to free yourself from the messes of life to let yourself serve the universe to the fullest extent. You have a power that many cannot even come close to. This is the power that not only changes you for the better but also the world around it.

Look at those around you and see what this journey has done for them. You are able to be present with them and help guide them to their own peace and fulfillment now. Your energy bursts with positive vibes and influence that the world craves, sharing it with everyone you meet. You are able to stand on your own two feet and defend them and everything you know to be right. There is no letting those around you take you down. You are finally a being who can handle whatever life throws at them, and then be able to throw it back.

<u>What Next?</u>

There is no more training. You are encouraged to keep practicing the elements and everything you have learned, though it's not as urgent as it was before. Just enough to keep your skills sharp and yourself in tip-top shape. Practice should look more like small daily habits and routines. It won't be enough to consume large amounts of time like your previous training may have looked.

Where you go and what you do now is entirely up to you. It is your legacy after all. Take time to celebrate the journey you took. Then jump right in with whatever is your first mission. The first mission you deal with may even come to you. The world knows what it needs, and choosing you as the Avatar was in its plans. It knows you are capable of providing the guidance the world needs. Do not doubt, but accept that you are ready, even if you don't feel like that.

You have the rest of your life now to show everyone why you are the Avatar. An entire life to make positive impacts on the world. To achieve and feel fulfillment. Live your life now in a way that will dictate what people will one day say about you when you are gone. Set up the world for the next Avatar to take over. Help bring peace and balance to the world as the bridge between everyone. You have much potential and power, now impact the world in the way you've envisioned.

Extra Resources

Suicide & Mental Health Hotlines

National Suicide Prevention Lifeline: (800) 273-8255
The Trevor Project (LGBTQ+): (866) 488-7386
National Suicide Prevention Helpline UK: 0800-689-5652
Canada Suicide Prevention Service: 1-833-456-4566

Meditation

Calm.com
The Meditation Bible by Madonna Gauding (Book)
Mindful.org

Chakras

The Chakra Bible by Madonna Gauding (Book)
Chakra Theory and Meditation with Paul Grilley (DVD)
Chakra Healing: A Beginner's Guide to Self-Healing Techniques that
Balance the Chakras by Margarita Alcantara

Wellness & Healing

Trauma and Recovery: The Aftermath of Violence--from Domestic
Abuse to Political Terror by Judith Lewis Herman

Index

About the Author

Ronald Boudreau is a graduate from Grand Valley State University with a Bachelor of Science in Theatre and a Minor in writing. Before that, he acquired an Associates in Business Administration at Bay de noc Community College. He has been fascinated and practicing success strategies since he took a class back in 2014. Ron continues to help those around him reach their full potential beyond his first published book by one-on-one coaching and his content online. For more information visit his website: ronaldboudreau.com